COLLEGE INSTRUMENTAL TECHNIQUE SERIES

STRING ENSEMBLE METHOD

**Beginning Class Instruction in
Violin, Viola, Cello and Bass**

SECOND EDITION

ARTHUR C. EDWARDS
University of California
Los Angeles

WM. C. BROWN COMPANY PUBLISHERS
Dubuque, Iowa

MUSIC SERIES

Consulting Editor

Frederick W. Westphal
California State University, Sacramento

Printed in the United States of America

String Ensemble Method

Contents

Preface ix

Preface to the First Edition xi

Introduction xiii

Parts of String Instruments 1

Comparison of Violin and Viola 2

Holding the Instruments 3

Playing Pizzicato 6

Holding the Bows 7

Tone Production 10

The Shift of Positions 12

The Vibrato 13

Suggestions for Class Procedures 14

Procedures for the First Lesson 16

Lesson One—Open Strings 18

Bowing Quarter Notes on Open Strings
Bowing Half and Whole Notes on Open Strings
Bowing Dotted Half and Quarter Notes on Open Strings
Bowing Eighth Notes at Tip and Frog on Open Strings

Lesson Two—Open Strings (cont.) 26

Bowing Eighth Notes at Tip and Frog on Open Strings
Bowing Sixteenth Notes at Frog, Tip and Middle on Open Strings
Alternate Crossing of Strings
Alternation of Down Bow and Up Bow Emphasis with Crossing of Strings

Lesson Three—Finger Pattern No. 1 34

First Whole Step—Photographs of Fingering
First and Second Whole Steps—Successive Up Bows—the Slur Across Strings

Lesson Four—Finger Pattern No. 1 (cont.) 42

First and Second Whole Steps and Half Step—II Position on Bass—Photographs
    of Fingering
Successive Up Bows

Lesson Five—Finger Pattern No. 1 (cont.) 48

Complete Pattern—II Position on Cello—III Position on Bass
II 1/2 Position on Bass—Legato Bowing—Slur on Same String

Lesson Six—Finger Pattern No. 1 (cont.) 54

Complete Pattern
Mixed Note Slurs
Successive Down Bows

Lesson Seven—Finger Pattern No. 2 58
  Complete Pattern—Photographs of Fingering
  Staccato—Long Note Slurs
  Syncopation

Lesson Eight—Finger Pattern No. 2 (cont.) 62
  Complete Pattern

Lesson Nine—Finger Pattern No. 3 66
  Complete Pattern—Photographs of Fingering—1/2 Position on Bass
  Normal and Stretched Fingering on Cello
  Detached Tones within Slur

Lesson Ten—Finger Pattern No. 3 (cont.) 72
  Complete Pattern
  Alternate Bowing from Frog to Tip

Lesson Eleven—Finger Pattern No. 4 74
  Complete Pattern—Photographs of Fingering
  Pause between Bow Stroke in Same Direction

Lesson Twelve—Combinations of Finger Pattern No. 1 77
  G Major—Bowing Practice in Quarter and Eighth Notes
  Staccato Note within Slur

Lesson Thirteen—Combinations of Finger Pattern No. 1 (cont.) 79
  D Major—Bowing Practice in Eighth and Sixteenth Notes
  III Position on Cello—Mixed Note Slurs

Lesson Fourteen—Combinations of Finger Pattern No. 1 (cont.) 81
  A Major—Bowing Practice in Alternating Quarter and Eighth Notes
  Staccato Notes Within Slur
  C Major—Bowing Practice in Alternating Quarter and Eighth Notes
  Double Stops on Violin
  IV Position on Bass

Lesson Fifteen—Combinations of Finger Pattern No. 2 86
  G Major—Bowing Practice in Slurring Notes of Equal Time Value
  C Major—Bowing Practice in Alternating Slurs with Separate Strokes

Lesson Sixteen—Combinations of Finger Pattern No. 2 (cont.) 88
  F Major—Bowing Practice in Slurring Notes of Unequal Time Value
  D Minor
  B-flat Major—Bowing Practice in Slurring Notes of Equal Time Value

Lesson Seventeen—Combinations of Finger Pattern No. 3 92
  F Major—Bowing Practice in Triplets
  Lifting Bow on Eighth Notes
  D Minor—Detached Note within Slurs
  F Major—Long Slurs

Lesson Eighteen—Combinations of Finger Pattern No. 3 (cont.) 95
  B-flat Major—Bowing Practice in Slurring Unaccented to Accented Notes

Lesson Nineteen—Combinations of Finger Pattern No. 3 (cont.) 98
  E-flat Major—Bowing Practice in 6/4 and 6/8 Meters

Lesson Twenty—Combinations of Finger Pattern No. 3 (cont.) 99
  A-flat Major—Bowing Practice in Alternating Down and Up Bow
    Accents and Slurs and Separate Notes

Lesson Twenty-One—Combinations of Finger Pattern No. 4 103
   A Major—Bowing Practice in Alternating Down and Up Bow Accents
   Weak to Strong Beat Slurs

Lesson Twenty-Two—Combinations of Finger Pattern No. 4 (cont.) 106
   E Major—III 1/2 Position on Bass—Bowing Practice in Alternating Down
     and Up Bow Accents and Separate Notes and Slurs

Lesson Twenty-Three—Mixed Finger Patterns 110
   G Major—Pizzicato—Playing Forte
   D Major
   G Major—Mixed Note Slurs

Lesson Twenty-Four—Mixed Finger Patterns (cont.) 113
   C Major—Playing Piano

Lesson Twenty-Five—Mixed Finger Patterns (cont.) 115
   F Major—Contrast Between Staccato and Legato
   C Minor

Lesson Twenty-Six—Mixed Finger Patterns (cont.) 119
   B Minor—Syncopation
   A Major—Playing Sixteenth Notes with Wrist

Lesson Twenty-Seven—Mixed Finger Patterns with Altered Tones 122
   A Minor—Playing Pianissimo

Lesson Twenty-Eight—Chromatic Progressions and Review 124
   G Major—Playing Mezzo Forte
   F Major—Interplay of Mezzo Forte and Piano
   G Minor

Lesson Twenty-Nine—Chromatic Progressions and Review (cont.) 127
   E-flat Major—Playing Fortissimo
   G Major—Playing Mezzo Piano, Crescendo and Decrescendo

Lesson Thirty—Chromatic Progressions and Review (cont.) 130
   A Major
   C Major—Lift Bow on Rests

Lesson Thirty-One—Third Position on Violin and Viola and Review 132
   F Minor
   D Major
   E-flat Major

Lesson Thirty-Two—Third Position on Violin and Viola and Review (cont.) 135
   F Major
   C Major—Practice in Crescendo and Decrescendo

Lesson Thirty-Three—Third Position on Violin and Viola, and Review (cont.) 137
   C Major
   B-flat Major

Appendix 141
   Minor Scales—Melodic Form
   Arpeggios—Major and Minor
   Reference Charts for Major Scale Fingerings and Positions

Index of Musical Excerpts 155

Preface

The author is grateful to the many string teachers over the country who during the past ten years have used this Method sufficiently to require eight printings. The basic format and sequence of material seems as valid and logical today as when the Method was written. In this second edition, therefore, only the scope of material has been amplified, strengthening certain finger patterns and other technical aspects to achieve a better overall balance of instructional emphasis. It is hoped that the larger selection and variety of material available to the instructor will stimulate increased interest of both instructor and students.

Preface to the First Edition

This method was developed for the college student who is preparing to teach music in the elementary or secondary schools. It is specifically designed for the usually required string instrument course which includes the techniques of Violin, Viola, Cello and Bass. A unique feature of the method provides an opportunity for the student to study these related instruments from one score, rather than from four separate manuals. Experiences with the score should promote an awareness and a better understanding of the technical problems of each instrument.

The accelerated gradation of material in this method is geared to the more mature student of college level. Consequently, the amount of material, its scope and difficulty afford possibilities for greater playing proficiency.

The study of each instrument becomes a complete musical experience. Excerpts from symphonic literature comprise the material in this method. As a result, a familiarity with the thematic material of great orchestral works is acquired while learning to play the instruments. The use of a single book for the study of all the instruments not only develops ability in score reading but also broadens the musical perspective of the student as he observes the overall form and harmony as well as the technical problems of each part. The skills of ear training and sight singing can be utilized advantageously in attaining correct intonation which depends so vitally on an aural comprehension of intervals and their relationships.

The printed material on Tone Production, The Shift of Positions, The Vibrato and Suggestions for Class Procedures should provide invaluable help to the teacher. Because the basic purpose of the string class at the college level is to prepare students to become teachers of the string instruments, it is important that these students not only gain facility in playing the instruments but also develop correct techniques in teaching procedures. The prospective teacher should realize that the educational processes and basic musical tenets of this college method will apply to the more elementary materials used in teaching children, with this important difference: the rate of progress will be slower and consequently, less material will be covered. A slower rate of progress, however, does not imply more emphasis on the analytical or mechanical aspects; rather, the complete musical experience itself must be the initial and final goal.

Introduction

A more rapid gradation and a greater selection of material provide:

1. An opportunity to gain a more advanced technical command of each instrument through the use of II, III and IV positions on Cello; 1/2, II, II 1/2; III, III 1/2 and IV positions on Bass; and III position on Violin and Viola.

2. Ensemble arrangements in two, three and four parts. Most pieces have easy piano accompaniments.

Left hand technique is logically presented through melodic material based on four different finger patterns. Each pattern is an ascending, diatonic group of five tones in whole and half steps:

1. The major scale approach is used because of its more general familiarity.

2. Each successive pattern is introduced:

   a. According to frequency of use and degree of difficulty.
   b. Through melodies, limited to one string, which are transposed to all strings in an ordered sequence.

3. The basic finger patterns are combined to form scales and melodies in nine major and six minor keys.

4. As most of the material consists of major scale groupings, arpeggios and some minor scales are not included in the main body of the method but at the end in the Appendix.

5. Specific fingerings, changes of positions, combinations of patterns and altered tones are isolated for preparatory finger practice.

Right hand bowing technique is given proper emphasis by:

1. Providing specific material to develop a flexible wrist and fingers.

2. Isolating particular bowing problems as they appear.

3. Presenting a variety of bowings with the scales.

Parts of String Instruments

THE VIOLIN AND ITS PARTS

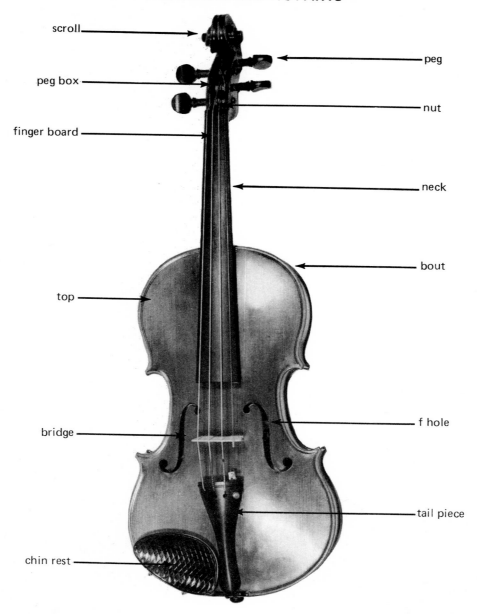

scroll

peg

peg box

nut

finger board

neck

bout

top

f hole

bridge

tail piece

chin rest

The parts of the Viola are the same as the parts of the Violin. The parts of the Cello or Bass are the same with this exception: instead of a chin rest, there is an adjustable pin that extends from lower end of instrument.

THE VIOLIN BOW AND ITS PARTS

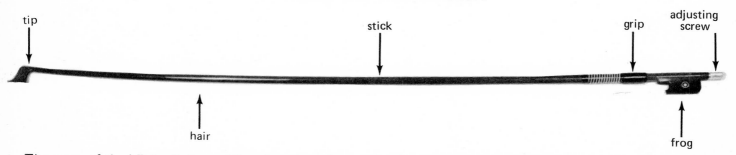

tip

stick

grip

adjusting screw

hair

frog

The parts of the Viola, Cello and Bass bows are the same as the parts of the Violin bow.

Comparison of Violin and Viola

The Viola bow is the same as the Violin bow except that the stick is slightly thicker and the frog, larger.

Holding the Instruments

HOLDING THE VIOLIN OR VIOLA

 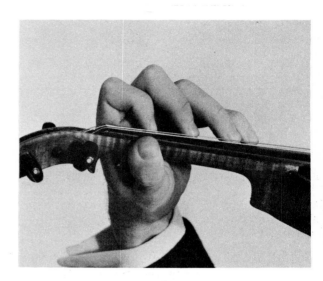

Place Violin or Viola on left side of collar bone.
Rest chin firmly on chin rest.

Suspend neck of instrument at eye level between base segment of forefinger and upper segment of thumb, which should be opposite the first finger or between the first and second fingers depending on the particular finger pattern; the middle joint of thumb should bend slightly outwards. If the instrument is supported with both the chin and the left hand, muscle tension is kept at a minimum.

If the player relies too much on the left hand to support the instrument, a shoulder pad may be used to facilitate a better grasp of the instrument with the chin. The particular shape of a shoulder pad or chin rest is determined by individual needs.

Hold left wrist away from neck of instrument in straight line with forearm.

Hold forearm under instrument with upper arm away from side of body.

Arch left hand fingers so that tips contact strings. Fingernails must be short enough to make this possible.

Keeping fingers on the strings, particularly the little finger, as much as possible in the beginning lessons will help set the correct position of the hand as well as the forearm under instrument. However, if this is overemphasized or continued too long it can retard the acquiring of finger facility.

Common Errors

- Neck of instrument drops into crotch between forefinger and thumb.

- Left wrist rests against neck of instrument.

- Left arm is held too far to the left.

- Left arm is relaxed to rest against side of body.

- Fingers of left hand contact strings on flat sides instead of finger tips.

3

HOLDING THE CELLO

Sit upright toward front of chair with left foot forward and right foot near chair leg.

Hold lower sides of instrument between knees with the upper back of instrument resting on chest so that instrument can be supported without assistance of left hand. Neck of instrument should be clear of any body support and scroll should be slightly above left shoulder. The end pin should be lengthened or shortened and set firmly on floor at the appropriate point to attain the correct holding position.

Place thumb of left hand on back of neck opposite second finger. Middle joint of thumb should bend slightly outward. This position of thumb and arching of hand will permit first finger to reach back and third and fourth fingers to stretch forward on finger board.

Keep fingers in an open or stretched position on finger board in order to reach both half and whole steps.

Arch left hand fingers so that tips contact strings. Fingernails must be short enough to make this possible.

Keep forearm in line with wrist.

Common Errors

- Right knee too far forward interferes with bowing on C string.
- Neck of instrument rests on left shoulder.
- Left thumb is raised on back of neck so that it is opposite forefinger.
- Left wrist rests against neck of instrument.
- Fingers contact strings on flat sides instead of finger tips.
- Fingers are in closed position so that first finger is too high (sharp) or fourth finger is too low (flat).
- Left arm is held too far up and out.
- Left arm rests on side of body or left upper bout of instrument.

HOLDING THE BASS

(See holding positions with French bow on page 10)

Stand erect with left foot placed diagonally to the left and with left knee slightly bent.

Rest instrument on end pin with upper back of instrument nearest player resting against inside of upper leg or thigh. When sitting, position of instrument should be basically the same (see photographs on p. 10).

End pin should be lengthened or shortened so that player can stand or sit erect and keep right arm straight, with bow resting about midway between lower end of finger board and bridge.

Raise or lower bow arm to level of each string when bowing while player's body remains erect.

Lean instrument a bit toward player to provide counter resistance in drawing up bows and thus help maintain a balanced position.

Place thumb of left hand on back of neck opposite second finger. Middle joint of thumb should bend slightly outward. This position of thumb and slight arching of wrist will permit thumb to act as a pivot and facilitate the reaching back of first finger and reaching forward of fourth finger on finger board to attain proper position of fingers.

Keep fingers in this open or stretched position on finger board at all times.

Keep fingers slightly arched with finger tips contacting strings in somewhat "flatter" position than on cello.

Keep left arm relaxed but away from upper bout of instrument.

Common Errors

- Player bends over front of instrument to bow on G and D strings.
- Instrument is held in vertical position so that up bow strokes tend to push instrument away from player.
- Left thumb is raised on back of neck so that it is opposite forefinger. This nullifies pivot action of thumb.
- Left wrist drops so that palm of hand grasps neck of instrument.
- Fingers are in closed position so that first finger is too high (sharp) and fourth finger is too low (flat).
- Left arm is extended too far up and out.
- Left arm rests on upper bout of instrument.

5

Playing Pizzicato

All instruments are held in usual playing positions. Bows may be placed on racks or held as indicated.

Pizzicato on Violin, Viola and Cello

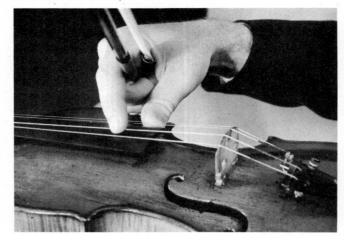 

Hold frog of bow in palm of hand so that forefinger and thumb are free.

Place tip of thumb against side of finger board near its upper end so that forefinger and bow are poised above strings.

Pluck string with fleshy tip of forefinger.

Pluck (or "pull") string from left to right so that it vibrates parallel to finger board and not against it.

Pizzicato on Bass

Hold frog of bow in palm of hand with little finger curled through frog and adjacent finger bent around stick.

Bow should point downward at side of finger board.

Pluck string with fleshy tip of first or second finger or tips of both fingers.

Pluck (or "pull") string from left to right so that it vibrates parallel to finger board and not against it.

Common Errors

- Pizzicato played too near bridge prevents free vibration of strings and produces poor tone quality.
- Pizzicato played with fingernail produces twangy tone.
- String plucked away from finger board causes it to touch finger board which interrupts vibrations.

Holding the Bows

HOLDING THE VIOLIN OR VIOLA BOW

A

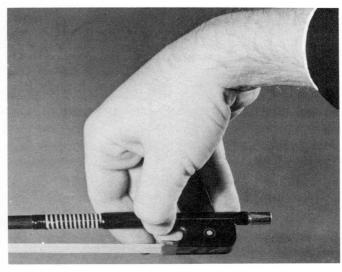

B

B

Grasp bow at middle of stick with left hand so that frog is to the right of player.

Place tip of slightly bent right thumb on underside of stick at point where inner corner of frog meets the stick.

Place second finger over top of stick with first segment opposite tip of thumb.

Rest tip of little finger on top of stick.

In the Russian method (A photographs), all fingers (except thumb) and wrist are inclined toward tip of bow so that middle joint of forefinger rests on top of stick; forearm and elbow are raised in line with upper hand.

In the Franco-Belgian method (B photographs), fingers are inclined less toward tip of bow so that middle segment of forefinger rests on side of stick; wrist is slightly arched and elbow is lowered.

The thumb underneath the stick and the second finger on top hold the bow; the upward pressure of thumb is countered by the downward pressure of second finger. The forefinger and little finger control the balance of bow.

Common Errors

● Tip of thumb rests in groove of frog.

● Thumb is stiff so that the flat of thumb instead of tip contacts underside of frog and stick. This may stiffen hand and wrist action.

● Bow is held by tips of fingers on top of stick, causing a flat, horizontal position of fingers and wrist rather than an inclined, vertical position.

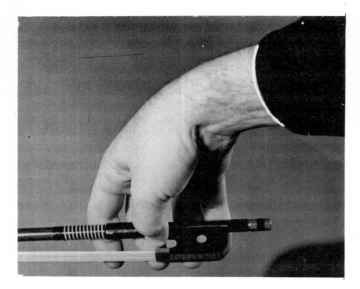
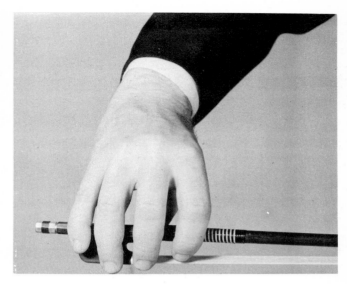

Cello Bow

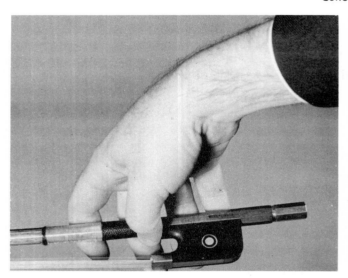
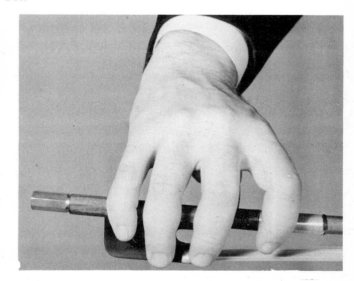

French Bass Bow

Grasp bow at middle of stick with left hand so that frog is to the right of player.

Place tip of slightly bent right thumb on underside of stick at point where inner corner of frog meets the stick.

Place second finger over top of stick and on side of frog so that middle segment of finger is opposite thumb.

Curve remaining fingers over top of stick in a vertical and slightly spread position so that middle segment of forefinger rests on side of stick, and third and fourth fingers rest on side of frog. Spread fingers a little more on Bass bow than on Cello bow.

> The thumb on one side of stick and second finger on other side hold the bow; pressure of thumb is countered by pressure of second finger. The other fingers control balance of bow.

Common Errors

- Tip of thumb rests in groove of frog.
- Thumb is stiff so that the flat of thumb instead of tip contacts underside of frog and stick. This may stiffen hand and wrist action.
- Bow is held by tips of fingers on top of stick, causing a flat, horizontal position of fingers and wrist rather than an inclined, vertical position.

HOLDING THE GERMAN BASS BOW

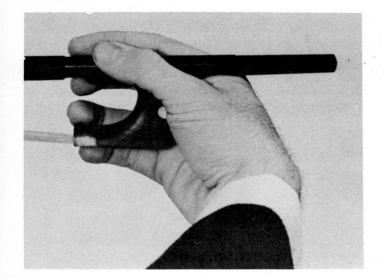 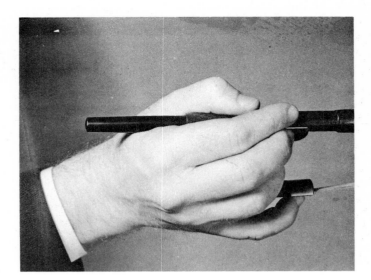

Grasp bow at middle of stick with left hand so that frog is to the right of player.

Place frog of bow in palm of right hand so that end of stick rests between thumb and forefinger.

Place thumb on upper side of stick almost on top.

Place forefinger on upper side of stick and second finger on upper part of frog.

Rest third finger on top of metal end of frog.

Rest tip of curved little finger on bottom of metal end of frog.

The thumb provides most of pressure on bow. The tips of first, second and little fingers control bow.

Common Errors

• Thumb is placed on side of frog.

• Bow is controlled by palm of hand and flat of fingers.

Tone Production

MOVEMENTS OF THE BOW

A   B

Down Bow (⊓) Movement from Frog to Tip

Grasp bow in correct holding position and place frog on strings halfway between bridge and upper end of finger board. This relationship of bow to bridge and finger board is fundamental to good tone production and should be maintained from frog to tip in both down bow and up bow movements.

The stick of Violin or Viola bow should incline away from player; the stick of Cello, French or German Bass bow can incline a bit toward player but generally, full (flat) contact of bow hair to strings should be maintained.

Violin, Viola, Cello or French Bass Bow:

When frog of bow is on strings, wrist should be arched upward (toward player's face on Violin and Viola) and in the Russian method (photograph A) the forearm is arched upward. In the Franco-Belgian method (photograph B) the forearm is relaxed downward but must never rest on player's side.

Little finger exerts sufficient pressure on top of stick to balance remainder of bow.

Bow is set in motion by slight flexing of wrist in down bow direction.

Bow is pulled for about two-thirds of its length as arch in wrist is gradually flattened. Control by little finger is gradually relaxed to middle of bow as forefinger assumes control.

For remaining third of movement to tip, bow is pushed diagonally outward. Pressure of forefinger on top of bow increases to tip to compensate for diminishing weight of bow.

At tip of bow on Violin and Viola, little finger may be pulled off of bow, depending on length of player's arm and fingers. On Cello and Bass, little finger remains curved over side of frog although it may be pulled up a bit toward top of stick.

German Bass Bow

When frog of bow is on strings, right arm should be straight but not stiff. Thumb exerts minimum pressure on stick because of weight of frog.

Bow is set in motion by slight flexing of wrist in down bow direction.

Bow is pulled from frog to tip, keeping right arm straight at all times. Thumb exerts increasing pressure on stick to compensate for diminishing weight of bow.

Because frog of bow is heavier than tip, the down bow stroke tends to impart more emphasis than the up bow. Therefore, the down bow should be used ordinarily on strong beats unless otherwise indicated.

Up Bow (⋁) Movement from Tip to Frog

Violin, Viola, Cello or French Bass Bow

When tip of bow is on strings, right arm should be straight and wrist flexed slightly outward.

To initiate an up bow, wrist anticipates the change of bow movement by a slight flexing in an up bow direction. This wrist movement provides a smooth change of bow.

Bow is pulled for about two-thirds of its length as wrist and arm are gradually arched upward.
Little finger gradually assumes more control of balance of bow.

For remaining third of movement to frog, bow is pushed back to its original position at frog.
Pressure of little finger is increased to balance increasing weight of upper part of bow.

German Bass Bow

When tip of bow is on strings, right arm should be straight. Thumb exerts pressure on stick to compensate for light weight of tip of bow.

To initiate an up bow, wrist anticipates change of bow movement by a slight flexing in an up bow direction. This wrist movement provides a smooth change of bow.

Bow is pushed back to its original position at frog, keeping right arm straight at all times. Right arm movement can be compared to a pendulum which swings freely from its top joint. Thumb gradually relaxes pressure to compensate for increasing weight of bow.

Because tip of bow is lighter than frog, the up bow stroke tends to impart less emphasis than the down bow. Therefore, the up bow should be used ordinarily on weak beats unless otherwise indicated.

Common Errors

Violin, Viola, Cello or French Bass Bow

● When frog of bow is on strings, wrist and fingers are flattened rather than in an arched position.

● Lack of elbow movement causes upper arm to move and results in bow movement which is semicircular rather than at right angles to strings.

German Bass Bow

● Elbow movement causes bow to move in semicircle rather than at right angles to strings.

● Fingers and wrist lack flexibility in bow movement.

● Tone is forced or scratchy because of:

Too much pressure of first finger at frog on Violin, Viola, Cello or French Bass bow, or of thumb on German Bass bow.

Too slow movement of bow.

Nearness of bow to bridge.

Insufficient tilting of bow so that too much hair contacts strings.

● Tone is thin or whistles because of:

Insufficient pressure of first finger on Violin, Viola, Cello or French Bass bow, or of thumb on German Bass bow.

Too rapid movement of bow.

Nearness of bow to finger board.

Too much tilting of bow so that not enough hair contacts strings.

The Shift of Positions

Definition of a Position

The group of pitches resulting from a single set placement of the left hand underneath the neck, and the fingers on the finger board of a string instrument constitutes a position.

The pieces through No. 12 (Lesson III) are in first position for all instruments. In the subsequent material, Bass and Cello (the latter beginning in No. 16) must change positions to match (on one string) the pitches of Violin and Viola.

Third position on Violin and Viola are dealt with in Lesson XXXI, however, the instructor may want to apply this position earlier (on these instruments) to other pieces in the Method.

Reasons for Shifting

Left hand is moved to a number of different positions on neck of instrument:

To extend range of each string.

To avoid awkward crossing of strings.

To retain tone color of one string within a phrase.

To facilitate fingering of a passage.

Indications of Shifting

Roman numerals are used in this book to indicate particular positions. If there is no Roman numeral, first position (I) is assumed.

A horizontal line following a Roman numeral indicates that particular position is maintained as long as the line continues or until different position is indicated.

Anticipation of Shifting

It is important that the student anticipate each change of position. He should learn to hear in his mind the first tone of the new position immediately before shifting.

Mechanics of Shifting

Basically, the shift is a movement of the whole left hand. Specifically, there is a gliding movement of the last finger used on the string to the first finger used in the new position. The movement should be made quickly, with a minimum of audible glide and without breaking the continuity of tone. A slight relaxation of finger pressure on neck and string at moment of shift will facilitate change of position.

If the shift is made with the same finger, it is accomplished by a quick glide of the finger to the new position.

If the shift is made from one finger to another, it is a combination of a glide of the finger in the preceding position with a leap to the finger in the new position.

In the shift to a higher position, the thumb and hand move at the same time as a unit. In the shift to a lower position, the thumb moves first followed by the hand but the two movements are so closely combined that they almost become a single movement.

In each of the positions, the relationship of fingers, hand and wrist to the neck of the instrument should be the same as for I position except that each new position occurs at a different place on the finger board.

Confidence in Shifting

In shifting, one must not be hesitant; rather, a bold and take-a-chance attitude is desired. The student may undershoot or overshoot the intended position, but eventually he will attain the "feel" of the correct distance.

Guide in Shifting

The student should depend mainly on his ear as a guide, rather than on a visual appraisal of distance. The first way is musical—develops an ear for intervals and facilitates reading; the second way is pedantic—depends on non-musical means and retards reading.

Isolation of Problems in Shifting

A smooth change of position is difficult and requires considerable practice in the beginning. It is suggested that when each shift of position occurs in the following material, it should be isolated and carefully practiced.

The Vibrato

When to Learn Vibrato

The vibrato is a means of adding expressive feeling and variety to one's playing. It may be learned when left hand fingers have attained a coordination and a "set" in their respective positions.

Mechanics of Vibrato

The vibrato is produced by a regular rolling movement of the fleshy tip of the finger on the string and in a parallel direction to it. The result is a recurring alternation of a slight raising and lowering of pitch. The oscillation should be a bit wider and faster when playing loudly and narrower and slower when playing softly.

On Violin and Viola the vibrato is a coordinated, rhythmic oscillation of wrist and fingers with the forearm following through each movement sympathetically. It is most important that the forearm move with the coordinated movement of wrist and fingers and not in the opposite direction. When correctly synchronized, the forearm will help accelerate, widen and establish regularity in the vibrato. When the forearm is moved in opposition, it will retard or even nullify the movement of wrist and fingers.

On Cello the vibrato is also a coordinated rolling movement of forearm, wrist and fingers but the forearm predominates. Because of the size of the instrument, the Cello vibrato is wider than the Violin vibrato.

The vibrato was not traditionally used on the Bass; however, it is now accepted as a part of the standard technique. The movements are similar to those of the Cello vibrato except that the oscillations are slower and wider, and more forearm is used.

How to Learn Vibrato

Place Violin or Viola under right arm so that left hand and arm action can be observed. The Cello or Bass player can observe his left hand and arm in his usual holding position.

Use correct vibrato movements as described on the previous page and practice with each finger separately in a very slow, controlled 2/4 rhythm (roll finger tip in one direction on count 1 and in the other direction on count 2).

Continue the preceding step but exactly twice as fast.

Continue the preceding step but again twice as fast.

Repeat the three preceding steps with instruments held in correct playing positions but without using bows.

Again repeat same three steps using long sustained bows; then, using shorter bows; and finally, using slurs with change of fingers on quarter notes in a moderate tempo.

Relaxation in Vibrato

There is a tendency in learning the vibrato to stiffen the fingers, wrist and arm muscles. Therefore, frequent periods of muscular relaxation are necessary.

Regularity and Speed in Vibrato

Regularity is more important than speed. A great deal of practice is necessary to develop a regular and semiautomatic vibrato at the right speed. If the movements are too slow, the effect will be offensive. If the movements are too fast, the effect will be strained or tight and likewise offensive. The vibrato is a highly individual means of expression and each player must develop his own characteristic speed and breadth of movement.

Suggestions for Class Procedures

Arrangement of Class

Each section of instruments should be near enough to the other sections so that each can rely on the mutual assistance of the class but still maintain its identity as a unit. A semicircular arrangement allows each student to observe as well as hear the other students. A separate stand should be provided for each student. There should be sufficient space between stands so that each player can bow freely and yet allow space for the teacher to move among the class and assist each student.

Tuning Procedure

In the beginning lessons, pizzicato should be used in tuning all strings except those of the Basses. To hear accurately the pitches of the Bass strings, it is necessary to use bows. To save class time, the Violins, Violas and Cellos should be tuned together. Begin with the A strings and progress to the D and G strings. When the A is sounded, it is very important that the players listen carefully, take a moment to think the pitch and then try to match it by turning the pegs while softly plucking the A strings. It will be necessary in the beginning to interrupt the tuning procedure, sound the A again, listen to it and again tune. After the Cellos and Violas have tuned their C strings, the E strings on the Violins should be tuned. Each Violin should have an additional E-tuner attached to the tail piece. This enables the student to make finer adjustments in the pitch of the E string. Cellos with steel strings also have tuners for finer pitch adjustments of these strings.

This procedure should be used at the beginning of each lesson until the students have attained the ability to tune in fifths while using bows. Eventually, the Basses should learn to begin with the A and tune at the same time as the other instruments. The pitches of the Bass strings can be heard more easily and tuned more accurately by playing harmonics. These can be produced by dividing a string into half or quarter lengths and touching these points lightly with a left hand finger as the bow is drawn lightly over the string. The screw and gear mechanism for tuning the Basses makes them comparatively easy to tune.

The Violin or Viola should be placed on left knee of player with scroll of instrument uppermost and strings facing player. One hand should rest on upper bout of instrument so that thumb of that hand is free to pluck strings. The other hand should be free to turn pegs. The Cello or Bass should rest upright on floor; otherwise, the tuning procedure is the same.

In tuning the Violin, Viola or Cello, it is important that counter pressure be exerted with one hand on the opposite side of peg box while peg is adjusted with the other hand. Otherwise, the peg may not set itself firmly but instead, will slip loose. Sometimes a peg is so set in the box that it cannot be moved to raise the pitch of the string.

In this case, the peg should be released by a backward turn and gradually pressed toward the box as string is brought up to pitch.

If a string is wound as closely as possible to the inner side of peg box nearest the handle of that peg, the string will form a wedge which will tend to hold the peg firmly in place.

If a peg slips or sticks, a special preparation can be applied.

When a loose string is tightened to its correct pitch, the bridge must be watched as the increase in string tension can bend the bridge toward the peg box. If this happens, the bridge should be straightened and pulled back to its vertical position.

Demonstrations by Teacher

Demonstrating a new or difficult technical detail is the most effective means of teaching each string instrument. Pictures and verbal descriptions are helpful but a skilled demonstration clarifies through motion and sound pertinent technical aspects which afford stronger motivation and musical inspiration.

Relaxation Periods

It is important, especially in the beginning lessons, to plan several brief rest periods for students to relax muscles that have become tense from holding unusual positions. The instruments should be put down and each student should shake his arms, wrists and fingers from his shoulders until all muscles have become relaxed.

Use of Pizzicato

In introducing new material, it is helpful to play it first with pizzicato and later with the bow. This enables the student to focus more attention on left hand problems.

The Bow

Tighten adjusting screw so that the hair becomes taut enough to draw a firm bow stroke without the stick touching the strings. The bow should retain its natural inward curve. After playing, it is important to release the tension of bow hair. Rosin should be rubbed on bow hair occasionally to increase the hair's grasp of strings when bowing.

Thinking and Listening

Learning to think a correct pitch before fingering it is indispensable to developing accurate intonation and interval relationships. Specific measurements on the finger board of each instrument to attain correct intervals are mechanical, unmusical and retard the reading of notes. The guide of relative relationships of whole and half steps used in this method will assist the student as he listens carefully and adjusts his fingers to the correct pitches. Listening to other students play the same melody will improve intonation and increase rhythmic accuracy.

Ensemble Combinations

After the melody is learned, each ensemble part should be presented in unison as a countermelody. Because the melody and ensemble parts are interchangeable, different combinations should be used. When sufficient facility is gained, one or more students from each section may play in smaller ensembles.

Piano Accompaniments

Piano accompaniments supply appropriate harmonic background and musically enhance simple open string melodies. Listening to an accompaniment develops better intonation, and feeling the fundamental beat develops a stronger rhythmic sense.

Familiar Material

Review of familiar material which the class has learned to play and to enjoy has psychological importance in each lesson. Beginning with a familiar selection establishes a positive and confident attitude with which to progress to new material. For the same reason, it is wise to conclude each lesson with a familiar piece within the playing ability of all students. The feeling of accomplishment serves as the best incentive for continued interest and application.

Apportionment of Class Time

Because a specific skill is more readily acquired in several shorter periods of practice, material from previous lessons should be included in each class meeting. The attempt to master a piece or a specific problem in one class meeting demands persistent application for too long a period of time. Avoid the bugbear of all practice—monotony. In a 50-minute class meeting, the following division of time is suggested:

Tune instruments . . . . 5 minutes

Review one or two familiar pieces . . . . 5 minutes

Practice specific problems of previous lessons . . . . 10 minutes

Introduce new lesson . . . . 25 minutes

Review familiar material . . . . 5 minutes

Number of Class Meetings in a Semester

A class of two hour credits will usually:

1. Meet twice a week with instructor and practice individually for two hours without supervision, or
2. Meet four times a week with instructor and have a minimum of required outside practice. Supervised practice is recommended because:
   a. Incorrect positions and errors are found and corrected more quickly.
   b. Problems in transporting instruments are minimized.

Number of Instruments Studied in a Semester

The number of instruments studied and the amount of material covered depend on individual school requirements. The class should study and progress together as a unit, and all students should change instruments at the same time.

1. If the semester is divided approximately into thirds, the class can change instruments twice so that each student has the opportunity to study three instruments. A typical class of twenty should be divided into three groups: one of Basses, one of Cellos and one of Violins and Violas because the techniques of the latter two are so similar. After learning one instrument, the study of the others should progress more rapidly because of common technical problems and repetition of material.
2. If the plan is to change instruments once during the semester, each student should play either Violin or Viola for one half of the semester and either Cello or Bass for the other half. The class should be divided into approximately equal groups, e.g., five Violins, five Violas, five Cellos and five Basses.
3. If one instrument is to be studied by each student for the entire semester, a balanced grouping such as suggested above should be used.
4. In all of the above groupings, it is important that the notes of the alto clef be learned by their names as well as by their fingerings on the Viola. Many players and teachers still learn to read the alto clef by transposing Violin fingering.

Procedures for the First Lesson

The class should be arranged in sections and the instruments tuned.

The teacher should demonstrate the correct holding of the Violin, Viola, Cello and Bass. Each student then learns to hold his instrument correctly.

Actual playing should begin with pizzicato of open string pattern in No. 1 of Lesson I without using the music. While learning this pattern by rote, the student can concentrate on left hand and arm positions.

The teacher should demonstrate the correct holding and drawing of the bow on each of the instruments. Each student then learns to hold the bow and place it on the strings in correct positions.

In the second playing of No. 1, without music, the middle third of the bow should be used. At this time, particular attention should be given to correct bow positions and arm movements. This rote procedure not only helps to set correct playing positions but also establishes the relationships of group performance which are basic to group instruction.

The next and final step in the first lesson is to read the music of No. 1 again using the middle third of the bow. A facility for reading music will be developed only if the player learns constantly to watch the music as he maintains the correct playing positions by "feel."

At the conclusion of the lesson, be sure that each student loosens the hair of his bow, wipes off rosin from top of instrument with soft cloth, places his instrument properly in its case, and fastens the latches on the case.

Lesson One

OPEN STRINGS

1. Bowing Quarter Notes on Open Strings

Location of each open string (symbol, O):

Play exercise three ways: at middle third of bow, at upper third and at lower third.

When a part ends on an up bow, lift bow gradually from string as it nears the frog to release the tone smoothly.

19

2. Bowing Half and Whole Notes on Open Strings

Divide bow according to length of notes. Use a little more than half of bow for half notes and all of bow for whole notes.

Always move bow at right angles to finger board. Review principles of tone production on pp. 10-12.

3. Bowing Dotted Half and Quarter Notes on Open Strings

Use whole bow on each dotted half note; use less bow on shorter notes, moving bow faster on quarter notes and relaxing pressure slightly on bow.

23

4. Bowing Eighth Notes at Tip and Frog on Open Strings

Use wrist and finger movement primarily in change of bow on eighth notes although some use of forearm is necessary to keep bow at right angles to strings.

24

Lesson Two
OPEN STRINGS (cont.)

5. Bowing Eighth Notes at Tip and Frog on Open Strings

26

6. Bowing Sixteenth Notes at Frog, Tip and Middle on Open Strings

Use wrist and fingers in change of bow on sixteenth notes; avoid use of forearm.

The accent (>) is produced by increasing finger pressure on top of bow, then releasing the pressure with a quick movement of bow; the accent helps to group the sixteenth notes rhythmically.

7. Alternate Crossing of Strings

The forearm controls bow in a predominantly up and down movement on Violin and Viola, an in and out movement on Cello and an out and in movement on Bass. Avoid excessive movement of upper arm.

From *Symphony No. 5, First Movement*—Tschaikowsky

31

8. Alternation of Down Bow and Up Bow Emphasis with Crossing of Strings

Use predominantly wrist and fingers in change of bow on sixteenth notes, and forearm in crossing adjacent strings.

Use predominantly upper arm movement in skipping strings.

33

FINGER PATTERN NO. 1

Finger Pattern No. 1 consists of a first and a second whole step, a half-step and a third whole step.

As a guide to correct placement of fingers on strings, symbols of interval relationships between tones are used in the introduction of each pattern:

    The dash (——) between two tones indicates a whole step.

    The wedge (——) between two tones indicates a half step.

    Finger Pattern No. 1 is thus indicated: (—— —— —— ——)

On the opposite page are photographs showing all interval relationships of pattern on Violin and Viola, first three intervals on Cello and first two intervals on Bass.

Listening for the correct pitch rather than looking at the finger board will facilitate both the left hand technique and reading the score.

9. First Whole Step of Finger Pattern No. 1

Fingering on all instruments: O (open string), 1 (first finger).

Violin and Viola   Cello   Bass

10. First and Second Whole Steps of Finger Pattern No. 1

Fingering:

Refer to photographs of pattern on p. 35.

Violin and Viola—0, 1, 2. Major 3rd—2, 0.

Cello—0, 1, 3; the second whole step is fingered 1,3 because this fingering conforms best to the size of the average hand. Major 3rd—3,0.

Bass—0, 1, 4; the second whole step is fingered 1, 4 because this fingering conforms best to the size of the average hand. 3 is never used alone but always supports 4 so that 3 and 4 are used as a single fingering unit. Major 3rd—4,0.

To help establish correct hand positions in this and subsequent pattern exercises, place all fingers used in exercise on string and lift one at a time.

37

11. First and Second Whole Steps of Finger Pattern No. 1

In learning new material, it is helpful to play pizzicato and establish the fingering before bowing is introduced. This enables the student to focus his attention on one technical problem at a time.

Bowing:

Alternation of frog and tip of bow.

Successive up bows (V V): stop movement momentarily and then continue bow in same direction.

Duet Arrangements of 11.

12. First and Second Whole Steps of Finger Pattern No. 1

When there is a choice of two parts for each instrument, the Melody appears on the upper staff and the Ensemble part on the lower staff. To facilitate reading, indications of the Melody and Ensemble parts will be omitted in the following lessons. The entire class should practice Melody first, then Ensemble part, then divide into different combinations of parts.

To find beginning tone of Melody on each instrument, finger scale upward from open string.

Bowing:

The slur (♩♩ ⌒♩♩): all tones within a slur are played in a continuous movement of bow in one direction.

Crossing strings within a slur: use predominantly wrist and forearm.

From *Jupiter Symphony, First Movement*—Mozart

40

41

Lesson Four

FINGER PATTERN NO. 1 (cont.)

13. First and Second Whole Steps and Half Step of Finger Pattern No. 1

Fingering:

Refer to photographs of pattern on p. 35. Bass must change postions to complete the pattern on one string (see photographs on opposite page).

Violin and Viola—0, 1, 2, 3; 2 and 3 should touch on half steps. Consecutive fingers are used regardless of whole and half step relationships.

Perfect 4th—0,3.

Cello—0, 1, 3, 4; half steps are conveniently fingered by using consecutive fingers: 3, 4.

Perfect 4th—0,4.

Bass—0, 1 $^{II}\overline{2,4}$; II position extends range of string.

Remain in position as long as horizontal line continues.

Study material on shift of positions on pp. 12 and 13.

Practice the shift: 1, ^{II}2, ^{I}1.

Half step is 2, 4 and appears here in II position.

Perfect 4th—0, ^{II}4 and 0, 0 (skip string).

Bass

14. First and Second Whole Steps and Half Step of Finger Pattern No. 1

Fingering:

To find beginning tone on Cello and Bass, finger scale upward from open string.

Violin and Viola—Minor 3rd (A to C)—1,3.

Cello—Minor 3rd (A to C)—1,4.
    Perfect 4th (G to C)—0,4 (B to E)—3, 1.
    Perfect 5th (F# to B)—3,3.

Bass—Minor 3rd (A to C)—1, ᴵᴵ4.
    Perfect 4th (G to C)—ᴵᴵ$\overline{0, 4}$ (B to E)—1,1.
    Perfect 5th (B to E)—ᴵᴵ2,ᴵ1 (F# to B)—4, 1.
    Minor 7th (D to C)—0, ᴵᴵ4.

Bowing:

Play quarter notes with whole bows whenever possible.
Play eighth notes with quarter bows using predominantly wrist and fingers.

From *Valse Triste*—Sibelius

Bass

14. First and Second Whole Steps and Half Step of Finger Pattern No. 1

Fingering:

To find beginning tone on Cello and Bass, finger scale upward from open string.

Violin and Viola—Minor 3rd (A to C)—1,3.

Cello—Minor 3rd (A to C)—1,4.
   Perfect 4th (G to C)—0,4   (B to E)—3, 1.
   Perfect 5th (F# to B)—3,3.

Bass—Minor 3rd (A to C)—1, ¹¹4.
   Perfect 4th (G to C)—¹¹0, 4   (B to E)—1,1.
   Perfect 5th (B to E)—¹¹2,¹1   (F# to B)—4, 1.
   Minor 7th (D to C)—0, ¹¹4.

Bowing:

Play quarter notes with whole bows whenever possible.
Play eighth notes with quarter bows using predominantly wrist and fingers.

From *Valse Triste*—Sibelius

44

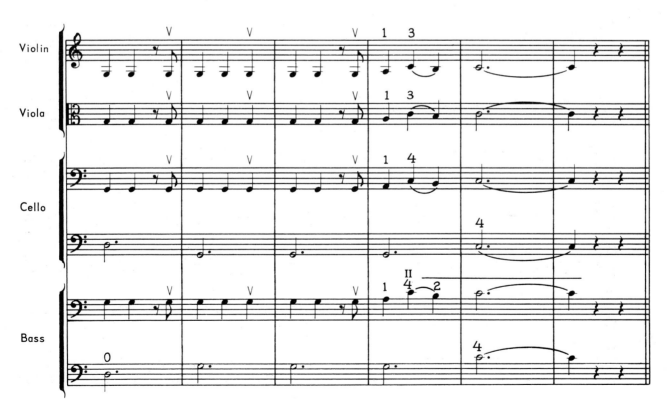

45

15. First and Second Whole Steps and Half Step of Finger Pattern No. 1

Fingering:

To find beginning tone on each instrument, finger scale upward from open string.

Viola and Cello can test beginning pitch in octave with next lower string.

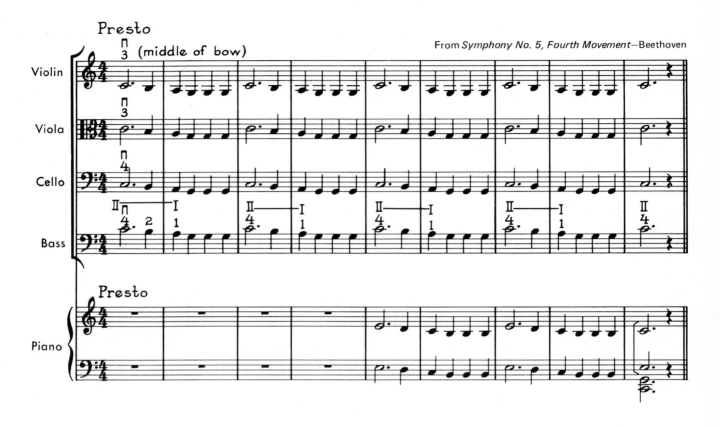

From *Symphony No. 5, Fourth Movement*—Beethoven

46

47

Lesson Five

FINGER PATTERN NO. 1 (cont.)

16. First and Second Whole Steps, Half Step and Third Whole Step
(Complete Finger Pattern No. 1)

Fingering:

Refer to photographs of pattern on p. 35. Cello and Bass must change positions to complete pattern on one string (see photographs opposite).

Violin and Viola—0, 1, 2, 3, 4, or 0; 4 and 0 produce the same pitch.
Perfect 5th—0, 4.

Cello—0, 1, $^{II}\overline{1, 2, 4}$; II position extends range of string.
Remain in position as long as horizontal line continues.
Study material on shift of positions on pp. 12-13.
Practice the shift: 1, ^{II}1, ^{I}1.
Whole step 2, 4 appears here in II position.
Perfect 5th (A to E)—0, ^{II}4.

Bass—0, 1, 4, $^{III}\overline{1, 4}$; III position extends range of string.
Practice the shift: 4, ^{III}1, ^{I}4.
Perfect 5th (G to D)—0, ^{III}4.

17. Complete Finger Pattern No. 1

Fingering:

Violin, Viola and Cello—4th finger varies tone color by producing pitch of open string (0) on different string.

Violin and Viola—Perfect 4th—1, 0 and 1, 4.

Cello—Perfect 4th—1, 0 and 1, ^{II}4.

Bass—II $^{1/2}$ and III positions retain tone color of one string. Half step is 2, 1 and appears here in II $^{1/2}$ position. Perfect 4th—1, ^{III}4.

Bowing:

Play legato which indicates smooth, continuous bow strokes; avoid breaking the tone in change of bow.

The slur:

From *Symphony No. 9, Second Movement*—Beethoven

50

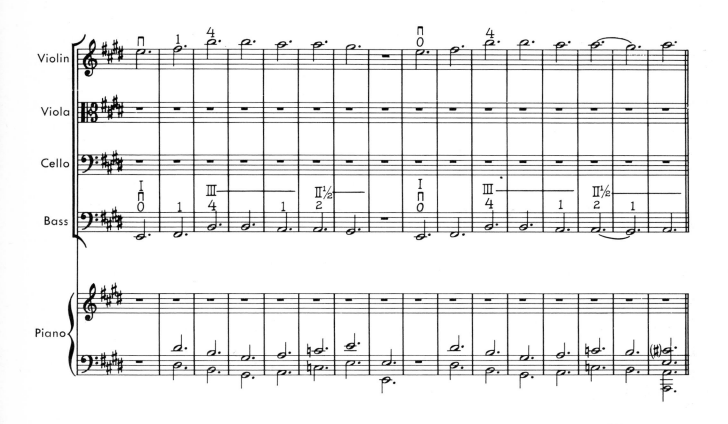

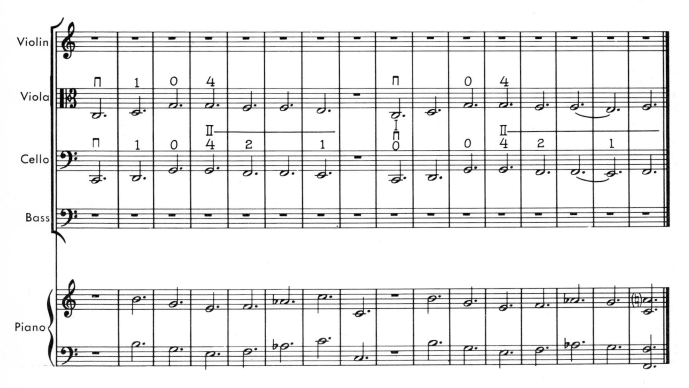

18. Complete Finger Pattern No. 1

Fingering

Violin and Viola—4th finger avoids awkward crossing of strings and retains tone color of one string throughout phrase.

Cello—II position avoids awkward crossing of strings and retains tone color of one string throughout phrase.

Bowing:

The slur: ♩ ♪ , ♫

Use long bows on slurs and long notes, and short bows on short notes.

From *Spanish Caprice*—Rimksy-Korsakoff

19. Complete Finger Pattern No. 1

Bowing:

The slur:

Bowing pattern can be practiced separately on open string.

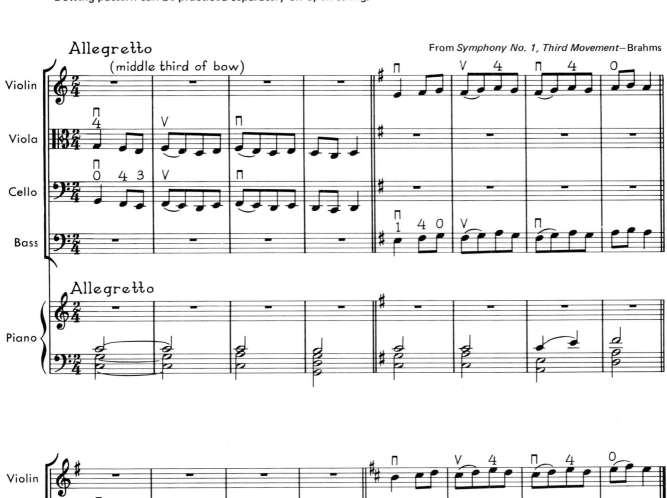

Allegretto

(middle third of bow)

From *Symphony No. 1, Third Movement*—Brahms

Allegretto

FINGER PATTERN NO. 1 (cont.)

20. Complete Finger Pattern No. 1

Bowing:

The rhythmic figure:

Ensemble Arrangement of 20

Fingering:

Violin—Minor 3rd (B to D)—2, 4.
   Major 6th (A to C)—4, 3.
   Major 7th (D to C$\sharp$)—0, 2.

Bass—Minor 3rd (C$\sharp$ to E)—4, 1.

Bowing:

The slur:

From *Haffner Symphony, Third Movement*—Mozart

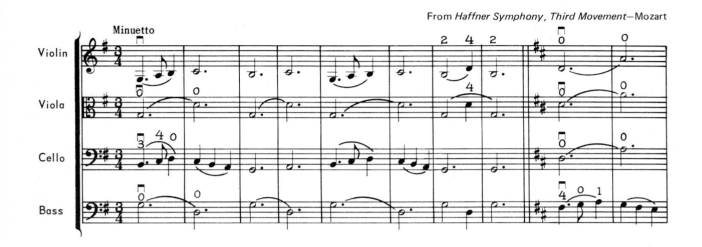

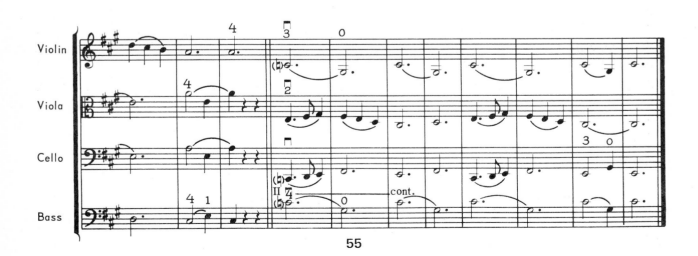

55

21. Complete Finger Pattern No. 1

Fingering:

    Violin and Viola—Minor 3rd (B to D)—2, 4.
        Perfect 5th (E to A)—1, 1. Roll finger across string.
        Major 6th (A to F$^\sharp$)—1, 2.

    Cello—Perfect 4th (D to A)—0, 1.
        Perfect 5th (E to A)—1, 1. Roll finger across string.
        Major 6th (A to F$^\sharp$)—1, 3.

    Bass—Perfect 5th (D to A)—0, 1.
        Major 6th (A to F$^\sharp$)—0, 4.

Bowing:

Successive down bows (⊓⊓): Lift bow on quarter rest and begin next down bow at frog.

From *Symphony No. 9, Fourth Movement*—Beethoven

56

57

FINGER PATTERN NO. 2

22. First Whole Step, Half Step, Second and Third Whole Steps
(Complete Finger Pattern No. 2, — ⌢ — —)

Fingering:

Complete pattern is shown in photographs on opposite page. Cello and Bass must change positions to complete pattern on one string.

Violin and Viola—Fingers 1 and 2 should touch on half steps.
   Major triad—4, 2, 0.

Cello and Bass—Half step of pattern: 1, 2.

Cello—Major triad—0, 3, 0 and ''4, 1, '0.

Bass—Major triad—'''4, '4, 0 and 1, 4, 0.

Left: Violin and Viola
Center: Cello
Right: Bass

23. Complete Finger Pattern No. 2

Fingering:

Violin and Viola—Major 3rd—2, 4.
   Major 6th—0, 1.

Cello—Major 3rd—2, ꞮꞮ4.
   Major 6th—0, 1.

Bass—Major 3rd—2, 1.
   Perfect 4th—1, 1, (cross strings with rolling movement of finger).

Bowing:

The slur:

Cello—Change of position within slur ꞮꞮ4, 2, Ꞽ2, 1.

Staccato—Indicated by a dot above or below note. Move bow with quick, short strokes keeping bow pressed firmly against string; separate strokes.

From *Symphony No. 5, Third Movement*—Beethoven

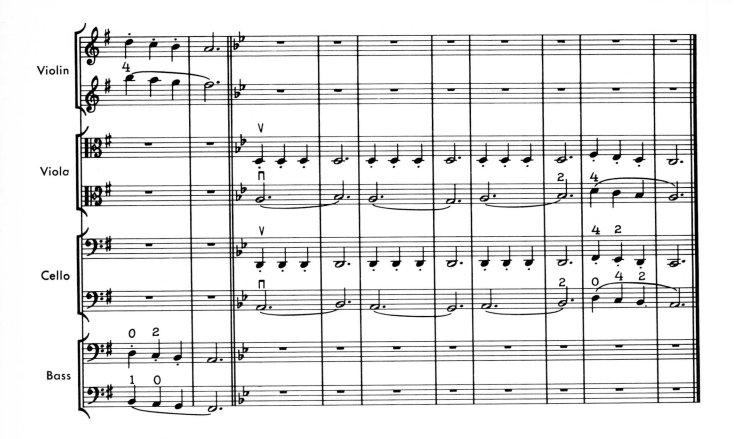

24. Complete Finger Pattern No. 2

Fingering:

    Violin and Viola—D minor triad—0, 2, 4.
    Cello—D minor triad—0, 2, 0.
    Bass—D minor triad—0, 2, 1.

Bowing:

    Syncopation.

From *Serenade for Strings, Fourth Movement*—Tschaikowsky

61

FINGER PATTERN NO. 2 (cont.)

25. Complete Finger Pattern No. 2

Fingering:
   Violin—Octave (B to B)—1, 4.

Bowing:
   The slur:

63

26. Complete Finger Pattern No. 2

Fingering:

Viola—Major 7th (E to F)—1, 3.

Cello—Major 7th (E to F)—1, 4.

Bowing:

Cello and Bass—Quick crossing of strings, back and forth.

From *Concerto for Cello, Second Movement*—Saint Saens

27. Complete Finger Pattern No. 2

Fingering:

Bass—Quick shift (A to C to A)—ᴵ1,ᴵᴵ4,ᴵ1.
　　　Minor 6th (C to A)—ᴵᴵ4,ᴵ1.

From *L'Arlesienne Suite*—Bizet

FINGER PATTERN NO. 3

28. First Half Step, First and Second Whole Steps,
Second Half Step or Third Whole Step
(Complete Finger Pattern No. 3, ⌢ — — ⌢ (—))

Fingering:

Whether final interval of pattern is half or whole step depends on key.
Complete pattern is shown in pictures on opposite page.

Violin and Viola—Arch finger 1 and keep it close to nut in first half step.
Cello—First half step: 0, 1.
   In first whole step, stretch between fingers 1 and 2. Remember to keep thumb opposite second finger.
   Second half step 2, 3 appears here in II position.
   II position facilitates fingering in flat keys.

Bass—First half step: 0, 1/2 1.
   1/2 position facilitates fingering in flat keys.

Left: Violin and Viola
Center: Cello
Right: Bass

29. First Half Step and First Whole Step of Finger Pattern No. 3

Fingering:

Cello—Stretched fingering for first whole step (1, 2) facilitates shift to II position.

The choice of normal or stretched fingering (1, 3, or 1, 2) is determined by the particular grouping of tones.

Allegro

From *Symphony No. 4, Third Movement*—Tschaikowsky

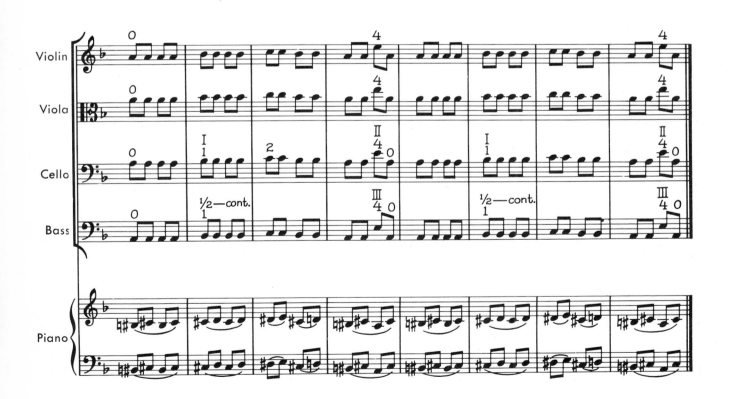

30. Complete Finger Pattern No. 3

Fingering:

Violin, Viola and Cello—Perfect 4th (B♭ to E♭)—2, 1.

Perfect 5th (F to B♭)—2, 2, (cross strings with rolling movement of finger).

Bass—Perfect 5th (F to B♭)—$^{1/2}$ $\overline{4,1}$.

Bowing:

The slur:

Detached tones within a slur:

Stop bow momentarily between tones and then continue bow in same direction.

From *Russian Easter Overture*—Rimsky-Korsakoff

71

FINGER PATTERN NO. 3 (cont.)

31. Complete Finger Pattern No. 3

Fingering:

Cello—Practice B$\flat$ ('3) to C ('' 3) to B$\flat$ ('3).

Bowing: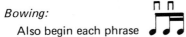

Also begin each phrase

From *Midsummer Night's Dream, Intermezzo*—Mendelssohn

32. Complete Finger Pattern No. 3

Fingering:

Cello—Stretched position between fingers 1 and 2.

Practice E♭ (¹2) to F (¹¹2) to E♭ (¹2).

Perfect 5th (D♭ to A♭)—1,1 roll finger across strings.

Bass—Perfect 5th (F to C)—$^{1/2}\overline{1,4}$.

Bowing:

Alternation from frog to tip.
Begin repetition with down bow.

From *Spanish Caprice*—Rimsky-Korsakoff

73

FINGER PATTERN NO. 4

33. First, Second and Third Whole Steps and Half Step
(Complete Finger Pattern No. 4, — — — ⌒)

Fingering:

Complete pattern is shown in pictures on opposite page.

Violin and Viola—Use extended finger 3 for third whole step. Finger 3 should touch finger 4 in half step.
   Major 3rd—1, 3.

Cello—In second whole step, stretch between fingers 1 and 2. Thumb remains approximately opposite finger 2.
   Major 3rd—1, 4.

Bass—Practice whole step fingering of $^{1}4$ to $^{1/2}1$ on adjacent higher string.
   Major 3rd—1, $^{II\ 1/2}4$.

Left: Violin and Viola
Center: Cello
Right: Bass

34. Complete Finger Pattern No. 4

Because the three successive whole steps tend to establish a whole tone scale, this pattern is used most frequently without the first whole step 0, 1.

Fingering:

Cello—Minor 3rd (C♯ to E)—$^{II}\overline{1,4}$.

Bass—Minor 3rd (C♯ to E, G♯ to B)—$^{I}4$, $^{1/2}2$.

From *Jupiter Symphony, Fourth Movement*—Mozart

35. Complete Finger Pattern No. 4

Fingering:

Violin, Viola and Cello—Perfect 4th (between phrases)—2, 1.

Bass—Perfect 5th (between phrases)—4, 1.

From *Symphony No. 2, Fourth Movement*—Sibelius

76

Fingering:

Violin and Viola—E Major triad—1, 3, 1.
Cello—E Major triad—1, 4, 1.
Bass—E Major triad—1, $^{II\,11/2}\overline{4,\ 1}$ (cross strings in
11$^{1/2}$ position).
Major 3rd (D♯ to B)—$^{1/2}\overline{1,\ 2}.$
Perfect 4th (B to E)—$^{1/2}\overline{2,\ 2}$ and $^{1/2}$2, ^{1}1.

Bowing:

The pause (,) and continuation of bow in same
direction.

From *Symphony in C Major, Third Movement*—Schubert

Lesson Twelve

COMBINATIONS OF
FINGER PATTERN NO. 1

37. G Major Scale

Bowing:

Practice scale these additional ways:

38. G Major

Fingering:

Cello—Perfect 5th (G to C)—4, 4 (cross strings with rolling movement of finger).

Bowing:

Play ♩♩♪ groupings at upper third of bow using predominantly wrist and fingers.

From *Symphony No. 6, First Movement*—Beethoven

39. G Major

Bowing:

Practice the following on open strings: ♩♩♩ ♩. ♩♩♩ ♩. (cont.)

From *Symphony No. 5, Fourth Movement*—Beethoven

78

Lesson Thirteen

COMBINATIONS OF
FINGER PATTERN NO. 1 (cont.)

40. D Major Scale

Fingering:

Bass—II position avoids skipping of intermediate string.

Bowing:

Practice scale these additional ways:

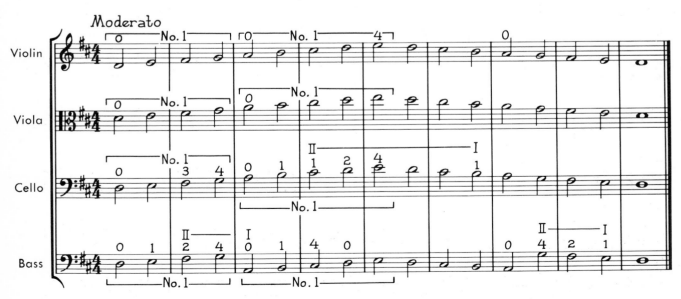

41. D Major

Fingering:

Violin and Viola—Major 3rd (G to B)—3, 1.
   Minor 7th (A to G)—1, 3.

Viola—Minor 7th (F♯ to E)—2, 4.

Cello—Two consecutive whole steps in III position
   (D to E to F♯)—1, 2, 4.
   Major 3rd (G to B)—4, 1.
   Perfect 4th (A to D)—0,ᴵᴵᴵ1 and (E to B)—ᴵᴵᴵ2,ᴵ1.
   Minor 7th (A to G)—1, 4.

Bowing:

The slur:

From *Symphony in E Minor, Second Movement*—Dvořák

80

42. D Major

Allegro

From *Surprise Symphony, Fourth Movement*—Haydn

Violin

Viola

Cello

Bass

Piano

Lesson Fourteen

COMBINATIONS OF FINGER PATTERN NO. 1 (cont.)

43. A Major Scale

This combination occurs only on Violin and Bass.

Bowing:

Practice scale these additional ways:

Moderato

Violin

Bass

44. A Major

Fingering:

    Violin and Viola—Octave (E to E)—4, 1.
      Major 9th (D to E)—0, 4.

Bowing:

    Staccato notes within slur: ; stop bow momentarily between notes and then continue bow in same
    direction.

    The slur: Bass—Change of position within slur.

From *Variations on a Theme of Haydn*—Brahms

82

83

45. C Major Scale

This combination occurs only on Viola and Cello.

Bowing:

Practice scale these additional ways:

46. C Major

Fingering:

Viola—Major 7th (C to B)—0, 2.
Bass—Find beginning tone from lower tones in
I position.
Change position on same tone (C to C)
III 1, II 1/2 2.
Crossing strings in III position simplifies
fingering. III (D)
Minor 3rd (C to A)—1, 4.

Cello—Major 7th (C to B)—0, 3.

Bowing:

Violin—For double stop, bow two tones on
adjacent strings at same time.

From *Slavonic Dances Op. 46, No. 1*—Dvořák

47. C Major

Fingering:

Cello—Minor 3rd (F to D)—^{II}2, ^{I}1.

Bass—Practice shift from C (^{II} 1/2 2) to D (^{IV} 1).
 Crossing strings in IV position simplifies fingering.
 Minor 3rd (D to B)—^{IV} $\overline{1,4}$.
 Perfect 4th (E to B)—^{IV} 4, ^{II} 1/2 1.

From *Midsummer Night's Dream, Intermezzo*—Mendelssohn

85

COMBINATIONS OF FINGER PATTERN NO. 2

48. G Major Scale

This combination occurs only on Violin and Bass.

Bowing:

Practice scale these additional ways:

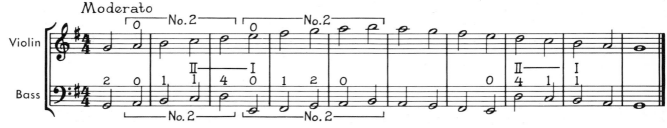

49. G Major

Fingering:

Violin, Viola, Cello and Bass—G major arpeggio.
Bass—Perfect 5th (G to D)—2, 0 (skip intermediate string).

From *Military Symphony, Fourth Movement*—Haydn

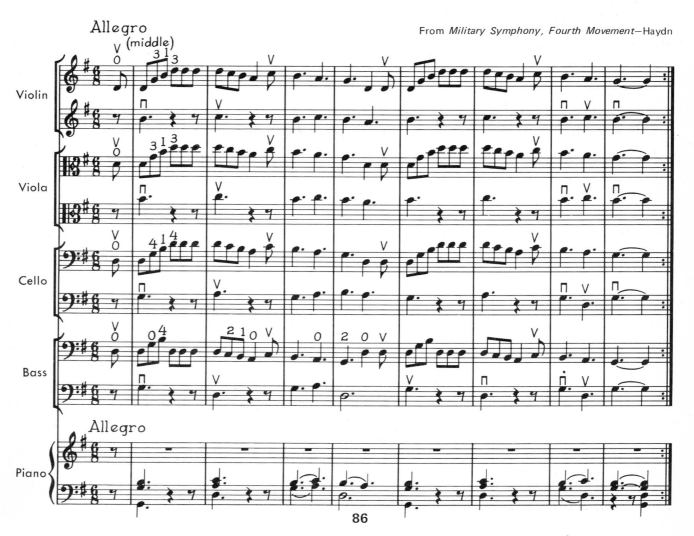

86

50. C Major Scale

Bowing:

Practice scale these additional ways:

Moderato

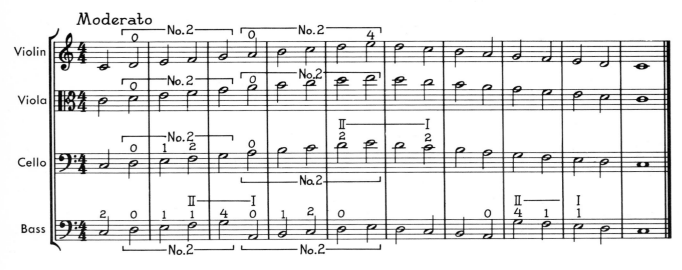

51. C Major

Fingering:

    Violin and Viola—Perfect 4th (G to C)—3, 2.
    Cello—Perfect 4th (G to C)—4, 2 and (B to E)—1, II4.
    Bass—Perfect 4th (G to C)—2, 2 (roll finger across strings.)
        Minor 7th (G to F)—2, 2 and (B to A)—1, 1 (skip intermediate string).

Bowing:

    Use wrist and finger movement on eighth and sixteenth notes.

Allegro

From *Serenade for Strings, Fourth Movement*—Tschaikowsky

COMBINATIONS OF FINGER PATTERN NO. 2 (cont.)

52. F Major Scale

Bowing:

Practice scale these additional ways:

53. F Major

Fingering:

Viola—Perfect 5th (C to F)—3, 3.
Cello—Perfect 5th (C to F)—4, 4.
  Minor 7th (C to B♭)—4, 1 (skip string).
  Octave (C to C)—3, 4 (skip string).

Bass—Perfect 4th (A to D)—1, ᴵᴵᴵ4.
  (G to C)—0, ᴵᴵ4.
Perfect 5th (F to C)—2, ᴵᴵ4.
  (C to F)—ᴵᴵ4, 1.
Practice shifts from C (ᴵᴵ4) to B♭ (ᴵ2).
  C (ᴵᴵᴵ1) to B♭ (ᴵ2).

Rhythm:
Change from ♩♩♩ to ♩♩.

Bowing:
Bass—Change of position (II to I) within slur.

From *Serenade for Strings, First Movement*—Tschaikowsky

54. D Minor

Fingering:

Violin, Viola, Cello and Bass—D minor arpeggio.
Cello—Minor 3rd (D to F)—0, ᴵᴵ1.
Octave (A to A)—ᴵᴵ4,ᴵ1.

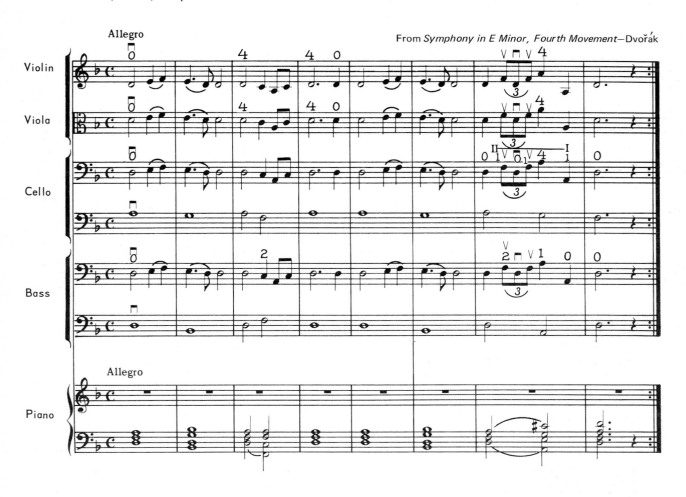

Allegro

From *Symphony in E Minor, Fourth Movement*—Dvořák

55. B-flat Major Scale

This combination occurs only on Viola and Cello.

Bowing:

Practice scale these additional ways:

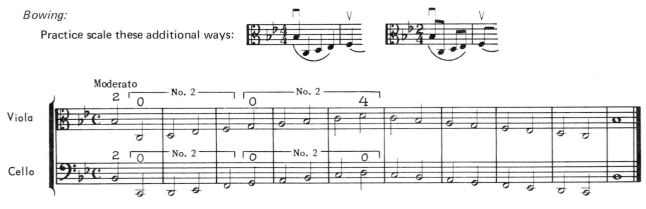

Moderato

56. B-flat Major

Fingering:

Cello—Octave between phrases (F to F)—2, 4 (skip intermediate string).

From *L'Arlesienne Suite, Farandole*—Bizet

90

COMBINATIONS OF FINGER PATTERN NO. 3

57. F Major Scale

Fingering:

Violin—Practice crossing strings from E(4) to F(1).
Viola—Major 7th (E to F)—4,2.
Cello—Crossing strings in II position simplifies fingering.
  Major 7th (E to F)—$^{II}\overline{4,1}$.
Bass—Minor 7th (E to D)—0,^{II}4.

Bowing:

Practice scale these additional ways:

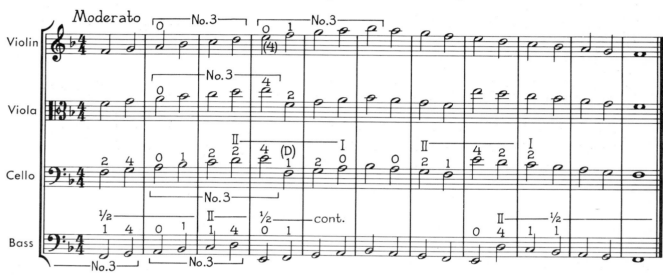

58. F Major

Fingering:

Bass—Perfect 4th (F to C)—$^{1/2}\overline{4,4}$ (cross strings with rolling movement of finger).

Bowing:

Practice two ways: Pizzicato and Arco, lifting bow on each rest.
Bass—In quick alternation of strings, use predominantly wrist and forearm.

From *Symphony No. 4, Third Movement*—Tschaikowsky

59. D Minor

Fingering:

Violin—Diminished 5th (G to C#)—2,3 (finger C# as D♭).

From *Peer Gynt Suite No. 1, Ase's Death*—Grieg

60. D Minor

Fingering:

Violin, Viola, Cello and Bass—D minor triad.
Violin—A minor triad.
Bass—Perfect 5th (D to G) $^{II}\overline{4,1}$.
Major 6th (F to D)—$^{1/2}1,^{II}4$.

From *Peer Gynt Suite No. 2, Solvejg's Song*—Grieg

61. D Minor

Fingering:

Viola—Major 7th (E to F)—4, 2.
Cello—Perfect 4th (A to D)—0, ^{III}1. .
   Minor 7th (F to G)—$^{III}\overline{4,1}$.
   Octave (F to F)—2,^{III}4.
Bass—Minor 7th (E to D)—0,^{II}4.

Bowing:

My Country (Symphonic Cycle) No. 2, *The Moldau*—Smetana

62. F Major

Fingering:

Violin and Viola—Perfect 5th (G to C)—3, 3 (cross strings with rolling movement of finger).
Cello—Practice whole step, B♭(1) to C (2).
   Perfect 4th (F to C)—^{III}4,^{I}2.
   Perfect 5th (G to C)—4, 4 (cross strings with rolling movement of finger).

From *Concerto for Violin, First Movement*—Beethoven

COMBINATIONS OF FINGER PATTERN NO. 3 (cont.)

63. B-flat Major Scale

Fingering:

Violin and Viola—Practice changes from A(4) to B♭(1) and E♭(4) to F(1).
Viola—Minor 7th (E♭ to F)—4,2.
Cello—Major 7th (D to E♭)—4,1.

Bowing:

Practice scale these additional ways:

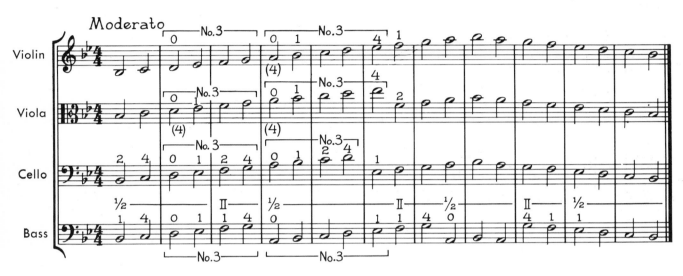

64. B-flat Major

From *Dance of the Buffoons*—Rimsky-Korsakoff

65. B-flat Major

Fingering:

Violin—Altered tone (E$^\flat$ to E$^\natural$)—4, 0.
Viola—Altered tone (C to C$^\sharp$)—2, 2.

Bowing:

Viola—Altered tone in slur (2, 2).
Cello and Bass—Syncopation.

From *Slavonic Dances Op. 46, No. 3*—Dvořák

66. B-flat Major

Fingering:

Violin and Viola—Major 6th (B$\flat$ to G)—2, 3.
Cello—Major 6th (B$\flat$ to G)—2, 4.
Bass—Major 6th (F to D)—$^{1/2}$1,^{II}4.
Octave (G to G)—$^{1/2}$4,^{II}4 (skip intermediate string).

Bowing:

From *Symphony in E-flat Major, Fifth Movement*—Schumann

97

COMBINATIONS OF
FINGER PATTERN NO. 3 (cont.)

67. E-flat Major Scale

Fingering:

Violin and Viola—Practice changes from D(4) to E♭(1) and A♭(4) to B♭(1).

Bowing:

Practice scale these additional ways:

68. E-flat Major

Fingering:

Cello—Minor 3rd (G to B♭)—¹¹3, ¹1.
Bass—Perfect 4th (B♭ to F)—¹/²4, ¹¹2.
    Minor 6th (C to A♭)—¹/²4̲, 1 (skip string).

Bowing:

Bass—Slur G(0) to A♭ (¹/²1) to B♭ (¹¹1).

From *Symphony in C Major, First Movement*—Schubert

Fingering:

Cello—Practice changes of position F(2) to G(ᴵᴵ2) and G(ᴵᴵ2) to F(ᴵ2).

Minuetto

From *Symphony in D Minor* (London), *Third Movement*—Haydn

Lesson Twenty

COMBINATIONS OF
FINGER PATTERN NO.3 (cont.)

70. A-flat Major Scale

Fingering:

Violin and Viola—Practice change from D♭(4) to E♭(1).
Cello—Combination of stretched fingering for whole step (1, 2) and regular fingering (1, 3).
  Practice change from D♭(ᴵᴵ4) to E♭(ᴵ1) and A♭(ᴵᴵ4) to B♭(ᴵ1)
Bass—Minor 7th (D♭ to E♭)—ᴵᴵ 1/2 4, 1/2 1.

Bowing:

Practice scale these additional ways:

Moderato

From *Russian Easter Overture*—Rimsky-Korsakoff

101

72. A-flat Major

Fingering:

    Cello—Practice position shifts of B♭ (^{II}1) to A♭ (^{II}4) and B♭ (2) to C(^{II}2).
        Minor 3rd (C to E♭)—^{II}3,^{I}1.
        Perfect 4th (E♭ to A♭)—1,^{II}4.
        Minor 6th (A♭ to C)—^{II}4,3.
    Bass—Practice position shifts of C ($^{II\ 1/2}$2) to B♭($^{1/2}$4) and B♭($^{1/2}$4) to C($^{II\ 1/2}$2).
        Minor 6th (A♭ to C)—$^{1/2}$1,4.
        Major 6th (E♭ to C)— $^{1/2}$1, $^{II\ 1/2}$2.

From *Midsummer Night's Dream, Intermezzo*—Mendelssohn

102

COMBINATIONS OF
FINGER PATTERN NO. 4

73. A Major Scale

Bowing:

Practice scale these additional ways:

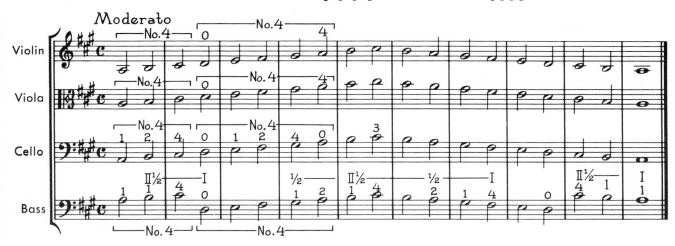

74. A Major

Fingering:

Bass—Perfect 4th (B to F#)—$^{II\ 1/2}$ $\overline{1,1}$.
  Perfect 5th (F# to C#)—$^{II\ 1/2}$ $\overline{1,4}$.

From *Overture to Romeo and Juliet*—Tschaikowsky

103

Fingering:

Cello—Minor 6th (A to C#)—0, 4.
Bass—Shifts of G#(1/2 1) to A('1) and E(1) to F#(II 1/2 1).
   Minor 6th (A to C#)—1, 4 (skip string).

From *Praeludium*—Järnefelt

76. A Major

Bowing:

Practice in slurring.
Bass—Change position in slur (G$^{\#}$ to E)—$^{II\ 1/2}$4,^{I}1.

Allegro

From *Concerto in B-flat Major for Piano, First Movement*—Tschaikowsky

COMBINATIONS OF
FINGER PATTERN NO. 4 (cont.)

77. E Major Scale

The final interval of the pattern, half step or whole step, is determined by the key.

Fingering:

Violin and Viola—Practice change from C# (3) to D# (4) to E(1).

Violin—Major 7th (G# to A)—3, 1.
Viola—Minor 7th (E to F#)—4, 2.
Cello—Practice change from F# (4) to G# (1) and C# (4) to D# (1).
Bass—Major 7th (D# to E)—III 1/2 4, I1.

Bowing:

Practice scale these additional ways:

Fingering:

Violin—Perfect 4th (G# to D#)—3, 4.
Cello—Minor 6th (G# to E)—1, 1 or 2.

78. E Major

Bass—Practice change from D#(1/2 1) to C#(I4).

Minor 3rd (F# to A)—II 1/2 1, III4.
Perfect 5th (G# to D#)—II 1/2 1, 4 (C# to F#)—II 1/2 1, I1.
Minor 6th (G# to E)—4, 1/2 2.

From *Tone Poem, Finlandia*—Sibelius

79. E Major

From *1812 Overture*—Tschaikowsky

80. E Major

Fingering:

Viola—Minor 2nd (A to A♯)—0, 1 (G to G♯)—3, 3 (C♯ to B♯)—3, 2.
Cello—Minor 2nd (B♭ to B♮)—1, 1 (A♯ to B)—1, 2.
    Diminished 3rd (G♯ to B♭)—4, 1.
Bass—Shift of positions from 1/2 to I.

From *Overture to Tannhäuser*—Wagner

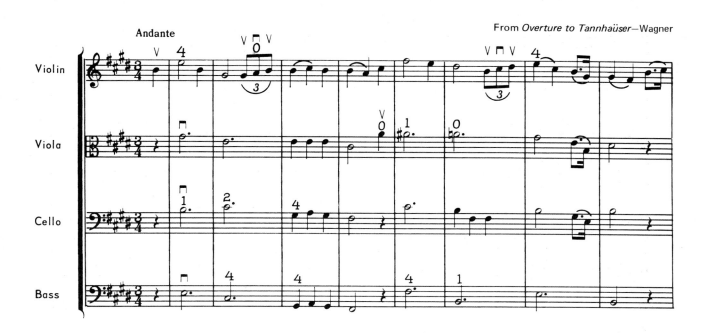

109

Lesson Twenty-Three
MIXED FINGER PATTERNS

81. G Major

Fingering:

Preparatory, silent practice.

Bowing:

Practice two ways: Pizzicato and Arco.

To produce dynamic, *f* (forte) indicating loud:

  1. Move bow near bridge using the flat or all of bow hair.

2. Violin, Viola, Cello—Increase pressure of first finger on top of bow.

  Bass—Increase pressure of thumb on top of German bow, or of first finger on top of French bow.

From Symphony No. 4, Third Movement—Tschaikowsky

110

82. D Major

Fingering:

Preparatory, silent practice.

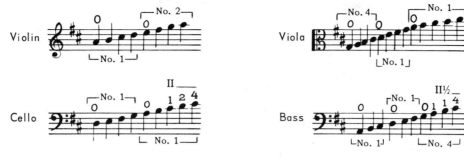

From *Water Music*—Handel

83. G Major

Fingering:

Preparatory, silent practice.

From *Military Symphony, Minuet*—Haydn

112

MIXED FINGER PATTERNS (cont.)

84. C Major

Fingering:

Preparatory, silent practice.

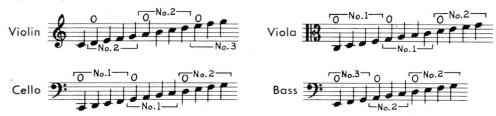

Bowing:

To produce dynamic, *p* (piano) indicating soft:

1. Move bow near upper end of finger board.
2. Violin, Viola—Tilt bow toward finger board using only part of bow hair.

Cello, Bass—Tilt bow toward bridge using only part of bow hair.

3. Violin, Viola, Cello—Relax pressure of first finger on top of bow.

Bass—Relax pressure of thumb on top of German bow, or of first finger on top of French bow.

From *Symphony in C Major, First Movement*—Schubert

85. C Major

Fingering:

Preparatory, silent practice.

Allegro

From *Symphony in C Major, Fourth Movement*—Schumann

MIXED FINGER PATTERNS (cont.)

86. F Major

Fingering:

Preparatory, silent practice.

From *Orpheus and Eurydice, Dance of the Happy Spirits*—Gluck

87. F Major

Fingering:

Preparatory, silent practice.

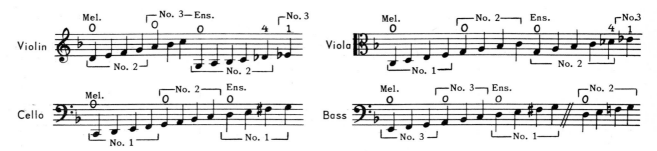

F major and C dominant 7th arpeggios.

Bowing:

Contrast between staccato and legato.

From *Surprise Symphony, Second Movement*—Haydn

116

117

88. C Minor

Fingering:

Preparatory, silent practice.

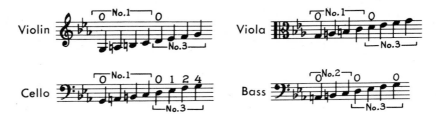

C minor arpeggio.

Lesson Twenty-Six
MIXED FINGER PATTERNS (cont.)

89. B Minor

Fingering:

Preparatory, silent practice.

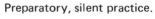

B minor arpeggio.

From *Russian Sailors' Dance*—Gliere

90. A Major

Fingering:

Preparatory, silent practice.

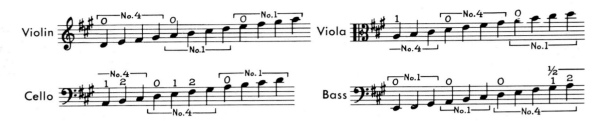

Allegro

From *Military Symphony, First Movement*—Haydn

91. A Major

Fingering:

Preparatory, silent practice.

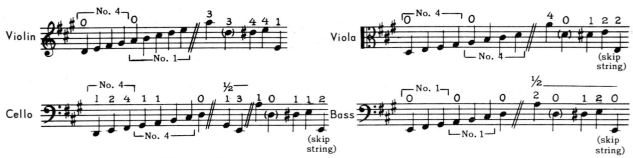

A major and C dominant 7th arpeggios.

From *Surprise Symphony, Second Movement*—Haydn

MIXED FINGER PATTERNS
WITH ALTERED TONES

92. A Minor

Fingering:

Preparatory, silent practice.

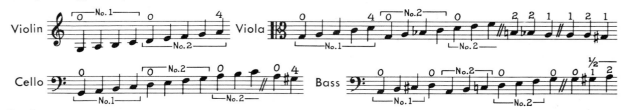

Bowing:

To produce dynamic, *pp* (pianissimo) indicating very soft:

1. Move bow in tilted position near upper end of finger board.
2. Use minimum finger pressure on top of bow.

From *Symphony No. 5, First Movement*—Tschaikowsky

93. A Minor

Preparatory, silent practice.

From *Symphony No. 7, Second Movement*—Beethoven

123

Lesson Twenty-Eight
CHROMATIC PROGRESSIONS AND REVIEW

94. G Major

Fingering:

Preparatory, silent practice.

Bowing:

To produce dynamic *mf* (mezzo forte) indicating medium loud:

1. Move bow near bridge using the flat of bow hair.
2. Increase finger pressure on top of bow.

From *Symphony in D Minor, First Movement*—Franck

124

95. F Major

Fingering:

Preparatory, silent practice.

From *Variations on a Theme of Haydn*—Brahms

96. G Minor

Fingering:

Preparatory, silent practice.

Moderato

From *Danse Macabre*—Saint-Saens

CHROMATIC PROGRESSIONS
AND REVIEW (cont.)

97. E-flat Major

Fingering:

Preparatory, silent practice.

Bowing:

To produce dynamic *ff* (fortissimo) indicating very loud:

1. Move bow near bridge using the flat or all of bow hair.
2. Violin, Viola, Cello—Apply pressure of first finger on top of bow.
   Bass—Apply pressure of thumb on top of German bow, and of first finger on top of French bow.

From *Dance of the Buffoons*—Rimsky-Korsakoff

98. G Major

Fingering:

Preparatory, silent practice.

Bowing:

To produce the dynamic *mp* (mezzo piano) indicating medium soft:

1. Move bow in tilted position near upper end of finger board.
2. Lighten finger pressure on top of bow.

To produce ——————◁ (crescendo) or increase in loudness:

1. Gradually move bow toward bridge.
2. Gradually flatten bow hair and increase finger pressure on top of bow.

To produce ▷—————— (decrescendo) or decrease in loudness:

1. Gradually move bow toward upper end of finger board.
2. Gradually tilt bow and decrease finger pressure on top of bow.

From *Symphony No. 2, First Movement*—Brahms

129

CHROMATIC PROGRESSIONS
AND REVIEW (cont.)

99. A Major

Fingering:

Preparatory, silent practice.

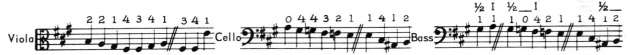

From *Prince Igor, Polovetsian Dances*—Borodin

100. C Major

Fingering:

Preparatory, silent practice.

From *Jupiter Symphony, Third Movement*—Mozart

131

Lesson Thirty-One

THIRD POSITION ON VIOLIN AND VIOLA AND REVIEW

Many of the following III position passages for Violin and Viola can be played in I position to develop familiarity with the interval successions. This procedure will often show the awkward fingerings or bowings of these passages in I position. As facility is developed in combining I and III positions, indicated on the score, the improved fingering and bowing which the III position provides will be more apparent.

101. F Minor

Fingering:

> Violin and Viola—III position extends range of string, avoids crossing strings and retains tone color of one string.
>
> Study material on shift of positions on pp. 12-13.
>
> Practice the shift of B♭('2) to C('''1) to B♭('2).
>
> Remain in III position as long as line continues.

From *Overture to Romeo and Juliet*—Tschaikowsky

102. D Major

From *Serenade for Strings, Third Movement*—Tschaikowsky

133

103. E-flat Major

Fingering:

Violin and Viola—The beginning tone is found on the A string in I position, then on the D string in III position.

Bowing:

III position simplifies bowing for Violin and Viola.

Alternation of staccato (at middle of bow) and legato.

From *Concerto for Cello, Second Movement*—Saint-Saens

THIRD POSITION ON VIOLIN AND VIOLA AND REVIEW (cont.)

104. F Major

From *Water Music, Air*—Handel

105. C Major

From *Symphony No. 5, First Movement*—Tschaikowsky

THIRD POSITION ON VIOLIN
AND VIOLA AND REVIEW (cont.)

106. C Major

From *Overture to Iphigenia in Aulis*—Gluck

Allegro

From *Slavonic Dances Op.46, No. 1*—Dvořák

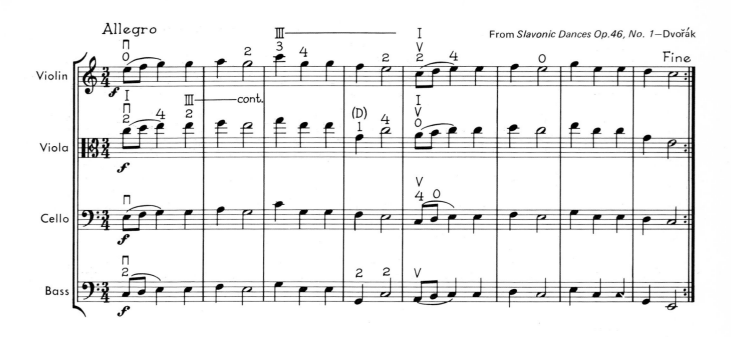

D.C. al Fine

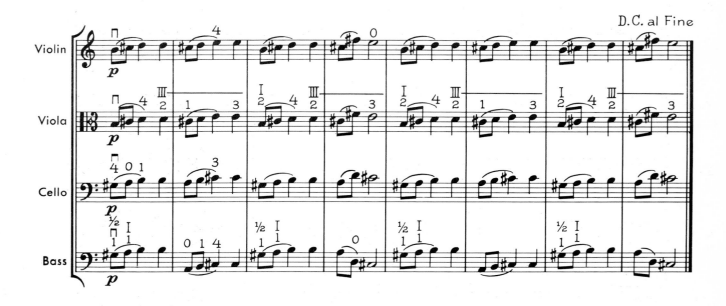

108. B♭ Major

From *Symphony in B-flat Major, Finale*—Schubert

139

Appendix

The major scales are included in the Method as they chronologically evolve from the combinations of finger patterns. Following, are the common minor scales (melodic form) and arpeggios utilizing the positions studied in the Method. The concluding Reference Charts are intended to help find specific fingerings of tones in various major keys and positions, however, these scales may also be used for practice by individual sections or instruments.

When III position fingerings on Violin and Viola are indicated they will be above the notes and I position fingerings, below the notes. All shifts of positions for all instruments can be practiced both ascending and descending according to the procedures on pp. 12-13.

Minor Scales—Melodic Form
(Using Positions Studied in Method)

G Minor

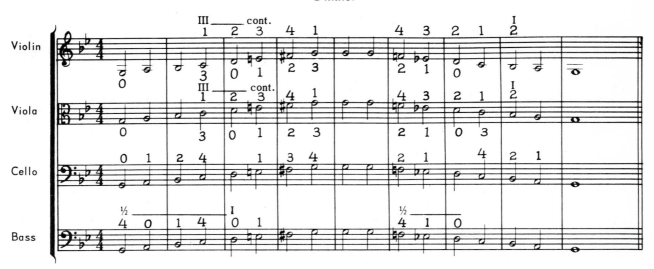

D Minor

A Minor

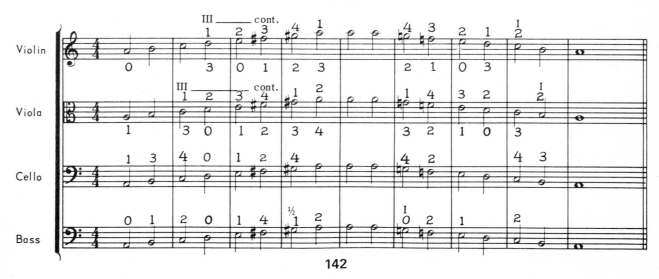

142

C Minor

F Minor

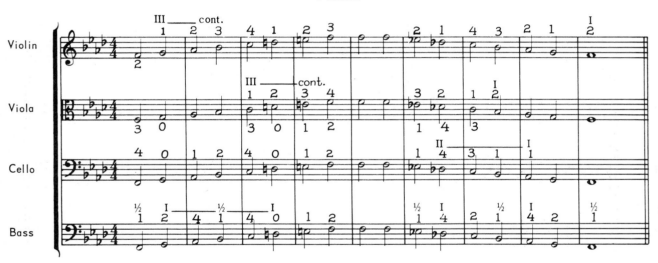

E Minor

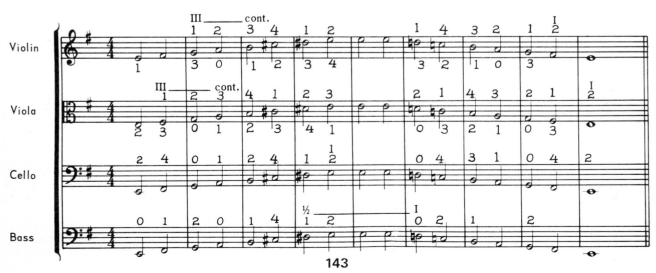

143

B Minor

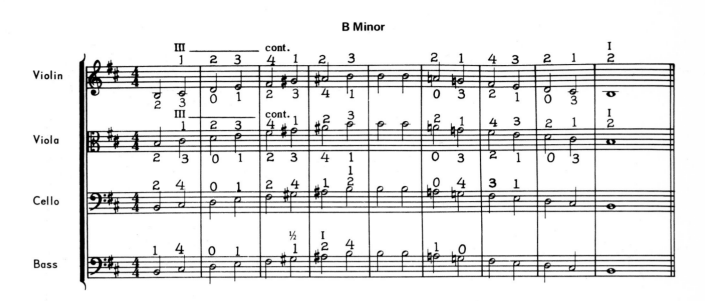

F#Minor

C#Minor

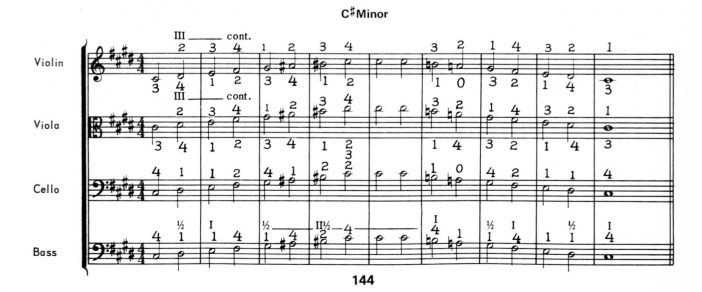

144

Arpeggios—Major and Minor
(Using Positions Studied in Method)

G Major and Minor

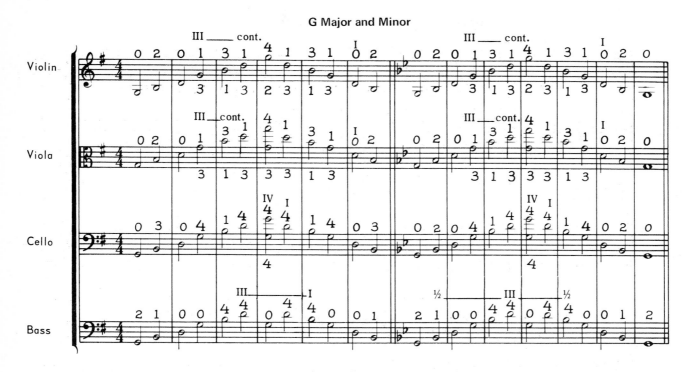

D Major and Minor

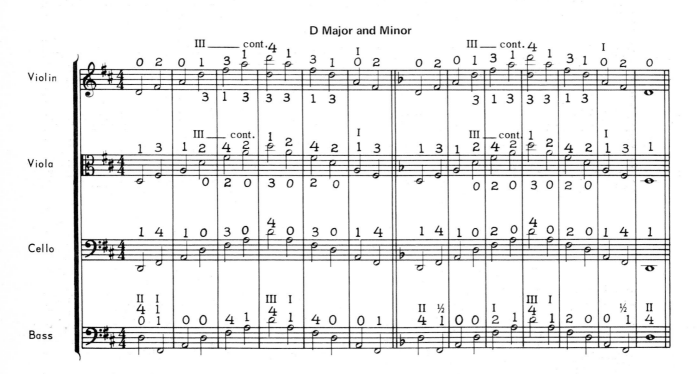

A Major and Minor

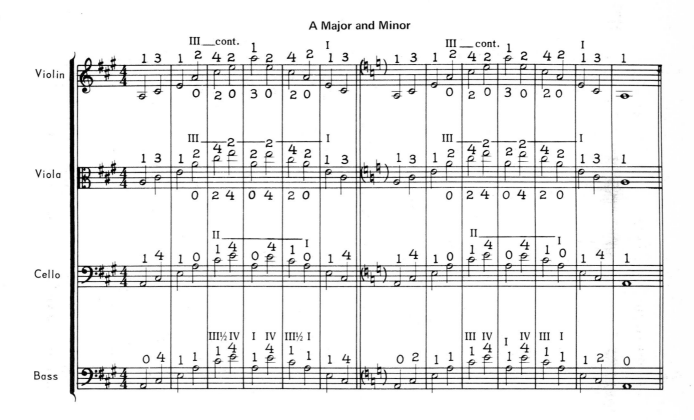

E Major and Minor

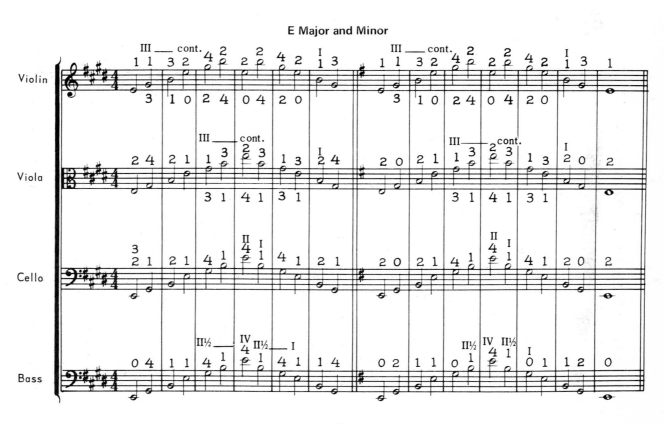

146

C Major and Minor

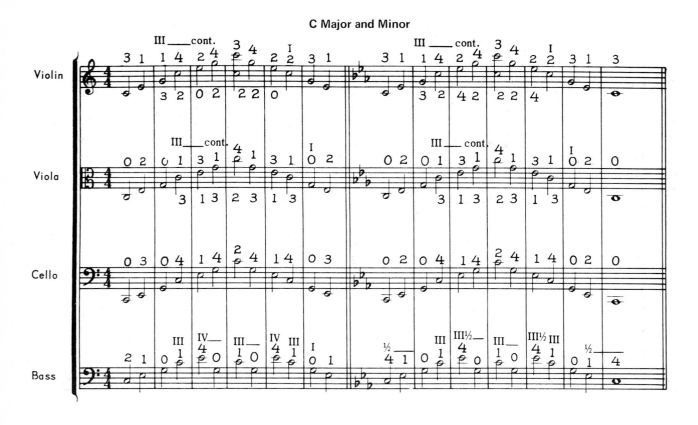

F Major and Minor

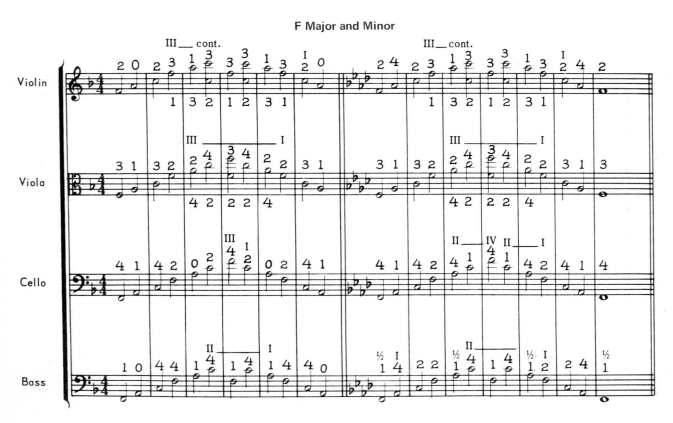

B Minor

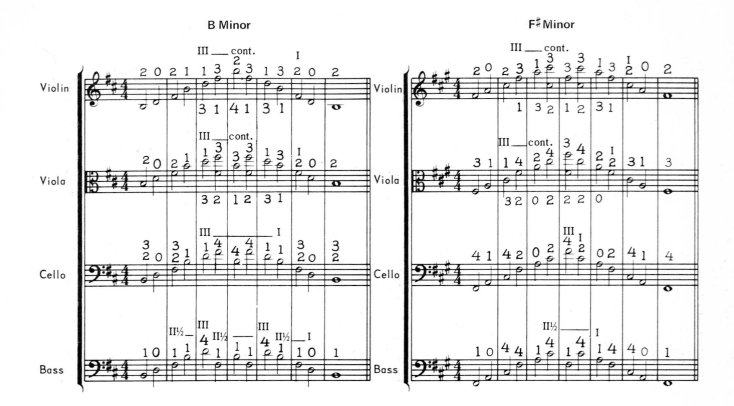

F♯ Minor

C♯ Minor

148

B♭ Major

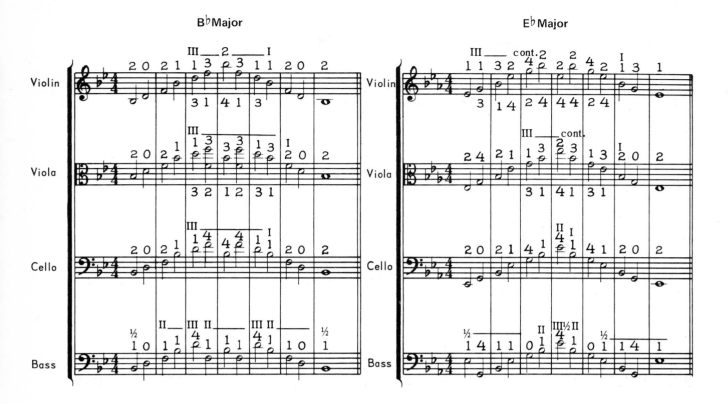

E♭ Major

A♭ Major

149

Reference Chart

Major Scale Fingerings for Violin
in I and III Positions

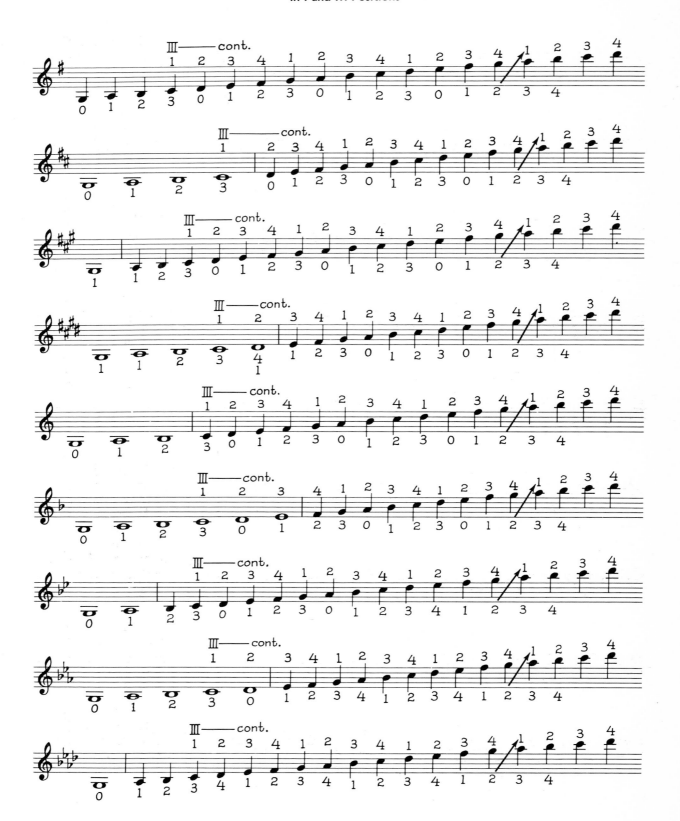

Reference Chart

Major Scale Fingerings for Viola
in I and III Positions

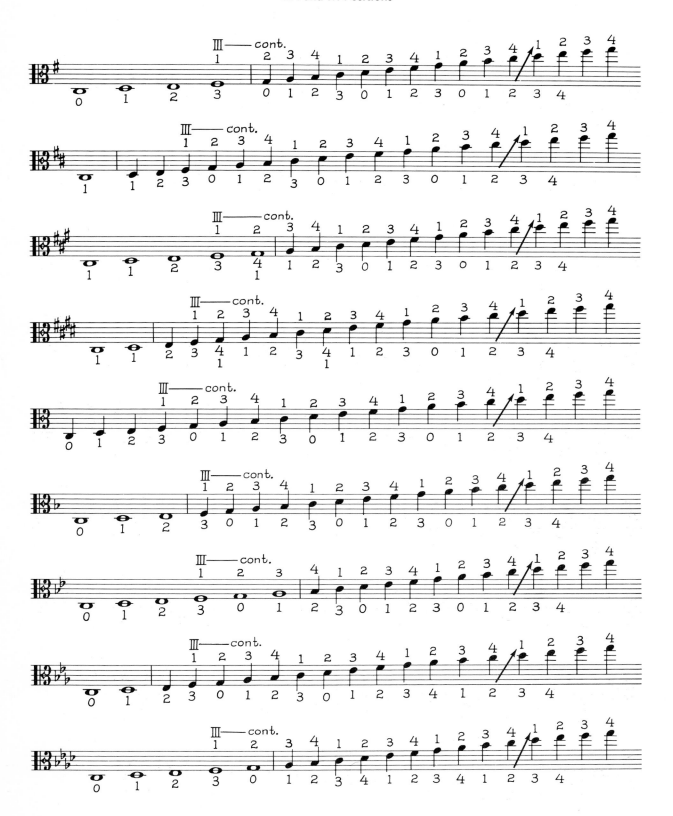

151

Reference Chart

Major Scale Fingerings for Cello
in I, II, III and IV Positions

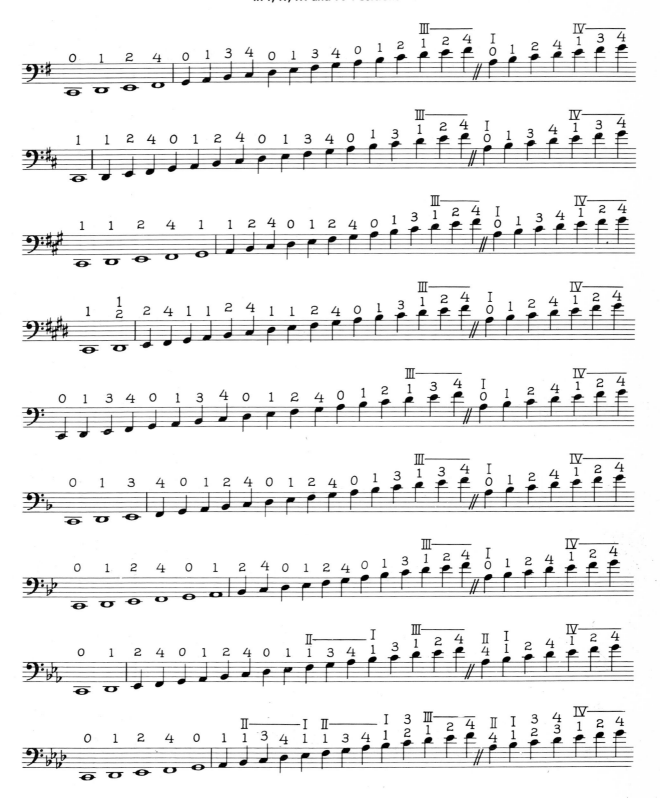

Reference Chart

Major Scale Fingerings for Bass
in I, ½, II, II½, III, III½ and IV Positions

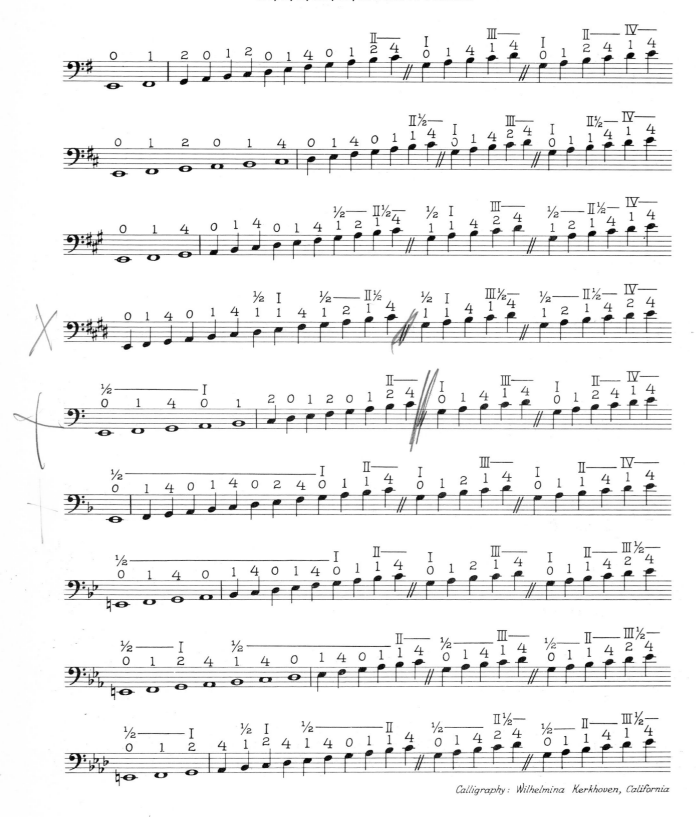

Calligraphy: Wilhelmina Kerkhoven, California

153

Index of Musical Excerpts

Beethoven, Ludwig Van	Concerto for Violin, First Movement	94
	Symphony No. 5, Third Movement	60
	Symphony No. 5, Fourth Movement	46, 78
	Symphony No. 6, First Movement	78
	Symphony No. 7, Second Movement	26, 123
	Symphony No. 9, Second Movement	50
	Symphony No. 9, Fourth Movement	56
Bizet, Georges	L'Arlesienne Suite, Adagietto	65
	L'Arlesienne Suite, Farandole	90
Borodin, Alexander	Prince Igor, Polovetsian Dances	130
Brahms, Johannes	Symphony No. 1, Third Movement	53
	Symphony No. 2, First Movement	128
	Variations on a Theme of Haydn	82, 125
Dvořák, Antonin	Slavonic Dances Op. 46, No. 1	84, 138
	Slavonic Dances Op. 46, No. 3	96
	Symphony in E Minor, Second Movement	80
	Symphony in E Minor, Fourth Movement	89
Franck, César	Symphony in D Minor, First Movement	124
Gliere, Reinhold	Russian Sailors' Dance	119
Gluck, Christoph	Orpheus and Eurydice, Dance of the Happy Spirits	115
	Overture to Iphigenia in Aulis	137
Grieg, Edvard	Peer Gynt Suite No. 1, Ase's Death	93
	Peer Gynt Suite No. 2, Solvejg's Song	93
Handel, George Frederick	Water Music, Allegro	111
	Water Music, Air	135
Haydn, Franz Josef	Symphony in D Minor (London), Third Movement	99
	Military Symphony, First Movement	120
	Military Symphony, Minuet	112
	Military Symphony, Fourth Movement	86
	Surprise Symphony, Second Movement	116, 121
	Surprise Symphony, Fourth Movement	81
Järnefelt, Armas	Praeludium	104
Mendelssohn, Felix	Midsummer Night's Dream, Intermezzo	72, 85, 102
	Overture to Midsummer Night's Dream	38

Mozart, Wolfgang Amadeus	Haffner Symphony, Third Movement	54, 55
	Jupiter Symphony, First Movement	40
	Jupiter Symphony, Third Movement	131
	Jupiter Symphony, Fourth Movement	75
Rimsky-Korsakoff, Nicolas	Dance of the Buffoons	95, 127
	Russian Easter Overture	70, 100
	Spanish Caprice	52, 73
Saint-Saens, Camille	Concerto for Cello, Second Movement	64, 134
	Danse Macabre	126
Schubert, Franz	Symphony in B-flat Major, Finale	139
	Symphony in C Major, First Movement	98, 113
	Symphony in C Major, Third Movement	77
Schumann, Robert	Symphony in B-flat Major, Fourth Movement	118
	Symphony in C Major, Fourth Movement	114
	Symphony in E-flat Major, Fifth Movement	97
Sibelius, Jean	Tone Poem, Finlandia	106
	Symphony No. 2, Fourth Movement	76
	Valse Triste	44
Smetana, Bedřich	My Country (Symphonic Cycle) No. 2, The Moldau	94
Tschaikowsky, Peter Ilich	Concerto in B-flat Major for Piano, First Movement	105
	Overture to Romeo and Juliet	103, 132
	1812 Overture	108
	Serenade for Strings, First Movement	88
	Serenade for Strings, Third Movement	132
	Serenade for Strings, Fourth Movement	61, 87
	Symphony No. 4, Third Movement	68, 92, 110
	Symphony No. 4, Fourth Movement	62
	Symphony No. 5, First Movement	30, 122, 136
Wagner, Richard	Overture to Tannhäuser	109